SOCIETY
AND
LOVE

SOCIETY
AND
LOVE

SOCIETY
AND
LOVE

Ethical Problems of Family Life

by

ROGER MEHL

TRANSLATED BY JAMES H. FARLEY

THE WESTMINSTER PRESS

Philadelphia

LIBRARY OF CONGRESS CATALOG CARD NO. 64–16349

Published by The Westminster Press®
Philadelphia, Pennsylvania 19107

PRINTED IN THE UNITED STATES OF AMERICA

FOR
*Idelette, Jean-Michel
and Clairette*

Contents

Part One: THE REALITY OF THE FAMILY

Part Two: LOVE AND THE LIFE OF THE BODY

Translator's Preface

Society and Love is one of the few books to approach the problem of love and family life from an informed Biblical standpoint, while at the same time taking into account the modern social situation of the family. It is hoped that the process of translation will not have obscured the important sociological implications of the work.

In certain respects the present translation is a literal one; no attempt has been made to paraphrase what the author has written. Professor Mehl has made his distinctions quite carefully, frequently with explicit philosophical, theological, or psychological terminology. Where no accepted English equivalents for such terminology have been available, the translator has chosen terms which, hopefully, express the sense of the original. In a very few instances French terms have been left, and the same is true in all cases where the author utilized foreign words. Certain of these words have become part of our current American vocabulary. In other cases the exact English equivalent would have been meaningless to the Anglo-Saxon reader, whereas an attempt to paraphrase would have branched off into commentary. In at least one instance the French word was so apt that the translator has anglicized it.

The major effort has been directed at forming sentences

and paragraph structure that would give maximum intelligibility in English to Professor Mehl's arguments and statements. Current American idiom utilizes more paragraphs and much shorter sentences than does French. Infrequently sentences have been rearranged; more often they have been broken up. In some cases nothing could be done to shorten the sentences without changing the meaning of the original.

Certain references in the book would have been obscure without translator's notes. Such notes have been kept to a minimum.

The translator would like to take this opportunity to acknowledge his appreciation to Professor Mehl, whose warm reception of the project of translation was greatly encouraging. He is also indebted to the members and the ministerial staff of Broad Street Presbyterian Church of Columbus, Ohio, for the material assistance necessary to survive the period of translation activity. Finally, he acknowledges the help of Mr. J. Robert Jacobson, who read the entire translation in its penultimate draft and who gave many valuable suggestions concerning style, grammar, and meaning, and the help of Miss Elizabeth G. Moore, who assisted in the preparation of the manuscript.

J. H. F.

Introduction

THIS BOOK is not intended to be an ethical guide for the family. No code for family life will be found in the pages that follow. What will be found there is simply a consideration of the meaning of the family, of the meaning of married life and of the presence of children. Law, as a matter of fact, is only a limit, the limit imposed on us from outside by an authority concerned with maintaining proper order. It is preoccupied with controlling the lapses of precisely those people who had not grasped the meaning of their existence in the family or in society. It is the function of law and of the state to restrict our undertakings by defining such laws as will hold the most senseless persons to respect the liberty of others.

Such is not the task of ethics. On the contrary, ethics aims at elucidating the meaning of all human situations as well as showing the diversity and richness that each human situation entails. In those places where the unrefined and perverted consciousness would have a tendency to see only brute and neuter facts — namely, the realities to which one must yield or which one can subdue if the power is available — ethics endeavors to bring out the human meanings. It seeks to make evident values that man can love and to which he can dedicate himself. The fam-

ily is certainly a sociological datum. Moreover, it is one
that has evolved in the course of history. But it is also the
bearer of a certain number of values that its juridical structures and monotonous banality are in danger of obscuring.
It is essential, then, to make an effort to bring out these
values once again.

Let us recognize that our task is remarkably facilitated
by one of the most important sociological facts of our age:
the rediscovery, in actual fact, of the meaning of the family, and the rediscovery, again in actual fact, of family ethics. At the outset of this essay of Christian ethics, we quite
willingly call upon a Marxist philosopher and sociologist,
Henri Lefebvre. In a conclusion to a survey organized by
the French Institute of Public Opinion and the weekly
journal L'Express on the New Wave (the younger generation should pay careful attention), Lefebvre remarked:
" Besides all aesthetic and ethical appraisals, the observer
of social facts should record a revaluation of the family.
It has been renovated and considered as a free association
between husband and wife. . . . Perhaps there is going
on around us, among these young people, what some soci-
ologists have ingeniously called a ' silent revolution.' This
renewing of an old institution could hardly get by without
negative aspects, in particular without a moralizing justification of new behavioral patterns. If it is true that an art
of happiness is being outlined, the ' values ' that will ac-
company it, that will protect it and justify it, can become
apparent only slowly. They will borrow the conformist
visage and the language of ancient values, old unmatched
garments that are still serviceable." [1]

It is precisely to this renewing of an old institution that
we would like to make our contribution in the present
book. This old institution, from time to time, has evolved

some questionable values. The family has been able to be
a hornet's nest. It has been able to have intimate partnership with a reactionary, paternalistic, and bourgeois social
order. It has been essentially a middle-class institution,
poorly adapted to other social classes. And we would be
the last to contest that there is a liberating wind in the
cruel words of André Gide: " Families, I hate you! "

The family is always, at one and the same time, a juridical and a social institution, a legal order and a human
community bearing particular values. It is normal only
when it presents these two aspects. However, these two
aspects have been dissociated, so that the family is nothing
more than what the marriage bureau and the judge are
able to see in it. But what is more, there is also a profound
disharmony between the family institution, with the ethical and juridical rules that govern it, and the living community of the married couple and the children.

This is, undoubtedly, how we should understand the
companionate-marriage crisis that deeply marked the first
four decades of the twentieth century. It is explained, in
large part, by this divorce between an institution characterized by masculine authoritarianism and paternalism and
by the fact that with equality woman became the companion of man.

The institution of marriage, under its civil form as under its religious form, and the community of marriage are
not related to the same values. The Christian reader will
allege, perhaps, that since the family and marriage are of
divine institution, and even prior to the Fall, they could
not change, and that it is shameful to envisage a reform of
the institution. This is only a regrettable play on words.
To say that the family is of divine institution is to say that
the life of man in the bosom of the family community is

in conformity with the divine will, and has a meaning in God's design regarding man.

This is in no way to affirm that the institution molded, for example, by the Napoleonic Code, and the various codes that have modified it, is the image of this will. The family has a history. In the course of this history it has evolved diverse values, in accordance with the various civilizations that have nourished it. That which the Old Testament tells us of patriarchal family organization is surely not applicable to the conjugal family of the twentieth century. This does not mean that these texts are null and void. The Word of God can still ring out through them. But if we try to find imperative models of organizations for our world in the different sociological realities to which Scripture makes allusion, we refuse to listen to the Word of the living God. The Word of God always makes itself understood through facts of history and human civilization, through sociological institutions. It never becomes identical with them. Can we say, for instance, that the bigamy of Abraham and the repudiation of Hagar have a normative value for us on the level of family ethics? And yet these facts have meaning for the understanding of the design of God.

These remarks will also explain why no statement of Christian principles will be found in the present work. An ethic composed of principles, no matter how general, is always headed toward legalism. Now, the Christian must live and think as a man freed from the law. In his family existence as in all his existence, the Christian cannot be subject to the law and thereby released from the responsibility of taking upon himself, in the presence of God, the conduct of his life. We should be glad that the state, as guardian of the public order, subjects the family to

principles and laws. The Christian will respect them. But
the demands of holiness and love cannot be set down in
principles and laws. They come to light, they assume
worth in our eyes, they become values for us only in the
encounter with God and with our fellowman. If an individual does not see his family life as an encounter of persons, if he does not have the concern to make his relationship with his spouse a personal encounter, each day more
complete and more transformed, he will be missing all the
values that are normally related to married life. And no
legislation will be able to compel him to discover them.
The values are given to us in our encounters with others.
It is always the encounter that is the mediator of values.
To propose a legalistic ethic is to wish to avoid as far as
possible this encounter and this mediation, just as a legalistic religion is always an attempt to avoid the personal
encounter with God, is always a flight from the presence
of God.

Our essay will merit the qualifier " Christian " not because of the Christian principles to which it would refer,
nor because of the number of Biblical citations to which
it will have recourse. Rather, it can be called a Christian
essay because of its refusal of all legalism, because of its
effort to understand the meaning of the values that are
given to us, for our good and our joy, in and by marriage
and the family.

Marriage and family undoubtedly create certain bonds.
They require a renunciation and definite choices. Marriage
is indissoluble. " What therefore God has joined together,
let not man put asunder." (Mark 10:9.) An ethic of marriage and the family is a Christian ethic to the extent that
it succeeds in recognizing in this marriage or parental
bond the sole occasion of our liberty. We like to place lib-

erty prior to the choice that binds us, or rather, at the moment of this choice. And we are not wrong in placing it there. But our liberty becomes meaningful only in the faithfulness to the commitment made. If the content of our commitments came down to a set of laws, if fidelity were submission to a law, then liberty would vanish and the married state would be slavery. It is assuredly this for many. And it remains this for each of us insofar as we do not discover the mysterious ties that exist between liberty and fidelity.

Religion also can become an insupportable tyranny when the covenant that unites us to God ceases to be a pact of fidelity and becomes a contract defining rights and duties. The subject of marriage and the family is the area of ethics where no legalism is possible, for it would discredit family and conjugal life forever. To respect the divine institution of marriage is to discover in it one of the most original expressions of liberty offered to the creature.

Our thought will develop in two phases. It will begin with the family community. It will analyze it, not being preoccupied with the family itself, considered abstractly, but with the family that exists in the middle of the twentieth century, which is placed in a particular social context and which suffers from the aftereffects of a long social evolution. It will seek to show the originality, in the present circumstances, of what Jean Lacroix has so aptly called "the family being."

This first reflection will bring us to a second stage. The married couple is founded on a carnal bond in which the totality of our person is engaged. This life of the body, as the expression of our personal life, as the expression of human love in its fullness, must also be the subject of an examination that discloses the meaning and the worth of it.

Part One

THE REALITY OF THE FAMILY

CHAPTER I

The Reality
of the "Social-Private" Sector

THE GENERAL title of this chapter, we should say right off, has a polemic intention. It takes aim at a certain form of individualism that has legitimately and progressively asserted itself on the political scene. This individualism goes hand in hand with a philosophical anthropology whose essential theme is the necessity of emancipating the human individual from all collective, tribal, and family bondage.

It is undoubtedly possible for it to seem anachronistic to put this individualism into question today. For in the course of our century a substantial and in many respects a disturbing reversal has taken place. Under the pressure of economic necessity, political individualism has widely given way. Even more, modern man, aware of his precariousness and his isolation, gives evidence of a nostalgia for community. This leads him to join in disciplined collectivities, which are often of a military style. But the paradoxical fact is that individualism has remained in its setting in relation to the family. The political ideologies that sought to root man deeply in the collectivity sought at the same time to free man, particularly the young, as quickly as possible from the family. Nazism, as well as communism, has given evidence of this. The theme of the family is considered as a reactionary theme.[2]

In our age there have been many attempts at community that have thought it possible to erect themselves on the breaking up of the family. The democratic movements of emancipation often have risen against the family. They have seen in it — legitimately enough, moreover — the origin and refuge of paternalism, of that typically bourgeois paternalism which has characterized the whole structure of our societies for several centuries. The employers of the great Western industrial community adopted this paternalism to their own advantage. It was against this that the trade union movements arose. The social achievements of these employers (e.g., those of the social — and Protestant — employers of nineteenth-century Mulhouse)[3] attest to the fact that in their eyes the workers were men destined to remain all their lives in the condition of children, of minors. The *employer* quite simply took the place of the *father*, just as in the former hierarchic society the king pretended to be the father of his subjects.

Thus Jean Lacroix was right[4] in linking the precariousness of the present-day family to a characteristic feature of our civilization, namely, the egalitarian tendency that expresses itself in a complex of hostility toward all authority and of guilt feelings toward these same authorities. This complex we might call, with the psychoanalysts, the murder of the father. It is quite possible that Lacroix is right when he attaches a decisive importance, in the evolution of Western spirituality, to the act of regicide. When the French people in 1793, having just proclaimed equality as a universal principle, sent to the scaffold their king, the father of the former subjects, they proclaimed at the same time their intention to fight against all forms of paternalism. This reaction had the same meaning as that of the adolescent who slams the door of the paternal home and who, secretly, awaits his liberation through the death of the father.

Our present-day societies, certainly, are more totalitarian than they are egalitarian. But even when their structures contradict their basic intention, they do not cease to display, in all good faith, a desire for the emancipation of man. The liberation of the proletariat, long considered as incapable of assuming its destiny itself; the liberation of the peoples of color kept in a minority state; the liberation of women with respect to the tutelage of marriage; the lowering of the age of majority for children — all these movements originate from the same impetus.

Our societies, then, find fault with any idea of hierarchy and authority, with anything that is regarded as being in conflict with the democratic ideal of equality and fraternity. Again, as Jean Lacroix remarks, everything takes place as if fraternity were incompatible with paternity. This rebellion of fraternity against paternity, which began with the murder of the king, was carried on in the fight against the employer. Will it not reach its fulfillment in the fight against the last potentate, the father of the family? The father is found to be more guilty than the king or the employer, for it is in the family that man becomes acquainted with authority. It is in the family that he can most easily receive the illusion that this submission is natural, that it is voluntary. Thus it is the family that makes a virtue of this surrender of rights. All that will discredit the authority in the heart of the family, all that will bring about total emancipation for the wife and children, will have as a consequence a considerable repercussion on the whole of social life.

And this explains why the political parties that are most

attached to the democratic evolution, real or supposed, of society are also the most impervious to problems concerning the family. Without doubt, they push to the vote measures that are aimed at the protection of the children in the family (family allowances, social security, medical supervision of all types, holiday camps). But these reforms, and we do not contest their legitimacy, do not necessarily signify a real attachment to the family institution or to the family being. Besides, all extraneous interference in favor of the family has, as an inevitable and legitimate result, a control over the family by the state. It brings, as a natural consequence, a blow to parental authority, a diminution of family cohesiveness.

This is, no doubt, a beneficient interference (we will have to discuss it). But is it obligatory that the substitution of an abstract and administrative authority for the concrete and personal authority of the parents be to the advantage of democracy, liberty, and fraternity? The question is too rarely posed. It is, however, worth posing. Let us be content, for the present, with remarking that our present-day societies, under their liberal democratic forms or under their collectivist democratic forms, and probably behind times in relation to the evolution of the spirit of the younger generations, have reactions of mistrust regarding the family. They do not grasp the positive meaning that the family can have.

It is proper, moreover, before justifying the family (not, to be sure, as a biological and nutrient-cell reality, but as a human community), to recognize that which is well founded in the negative attitude most often taken by modern political groups in regard to the family. It is by no means inexact to see in the family the source of paternalism and authoritarianism, even if it is not the only source. For the family is itself often conceived of as the *social cell*, following the formula frequently utilized by Roman Catholic thinkers and consistent with Roman Catholic doctrine. To say that it is the social cell means that it is the social reality that engenders or secretes all other social forms, endowing them, in the manner of an embryo, with its own structures. This view is based, no doubt, on historical grounds. For there has been a progressive passing from clans to empires. The clans were composed of families, in a way that historically the civil and religious society was constituted as a kind of expansion of the family or as a coupling of families. Are not the people of Israel the posterity of the family of Abraham? Social ties have been conceived on the model of family ties, the consequence of which has been, indeed, to deprive many men (to say nothing of women) of access to adulthood.

In fact, it is not correct to see the *present-day* family as the social cell, in the proper sense of the word. For this present-day family — the conjugal family — is far from being the matrix of other social structures. It is, on the contrary, at least sociologically, a residuum of social evolution. It has become increasingly restricted, more and more dominated and controlled, protected and, on occasion, threatened by the aggregate society that encompasses it. We will have to go into detail later concerning these ties of dependence which the family has in relation to society.

The family can merit the title of social cell only to the extent that it prepares its members for social life in an original and, in our opinion, an irreplaceable way. But this task, which is its own and which it does not always satisfactorily fulfill, does not authorize the family to extend its structures to the social body as a whole. Paternal authority, even reduced to a degree that does not compromise the personal dignity of the members of the family, is not something that can be exported. A fundamentally theological motive compels us to affirm the originality of the family: the Biblical account of the institution of the family presents it to us as the only social institution given to man before the Fall. Specifically human ties are set up in it that do not have equivalents in the social body. It is also true that the man who recognizes the blessing of having a father, of having been subjected to a father, is perfectly within his rights in denying other authorities paternal power of his person.

Certainly the phenomenon of social authority should not be challenged. Sinful man has need of being guided and of knowing that he is guided. But it is necessary for political and social authority to take more abstract, more institutional, and more legalistic forms, even if this causes it to lose something in benevolence and condescension. The entire movement for social and political emancipation has consisted exactly in bringing about the disappearance, as far as possible, of ties of personal independence, all of which recalled an unduly widespread paternalism. Institutions, by their abstract and impersonal natures, certainly limit one's liberty. But in subjecting the individual to a general law, they do not injure his personal dignity. They do not weigh on his innermost decisions. He can submit himself to them without being indebted to honor them.

All the social classes, including the proletariat, and all the occupational groups, including " household help " (formerly called " domestics," a name that is in itself significant), are progressively seeing to it that a status is guaranteed them which, by its juridical generality, prevents them from falling under the personal domination of any particular individual who would like to play abusively the role of father to them. It is through the obtaining of collective work contracts that workers have succeeded in overthrowing the very principle of employer paternalism, and have, at the same time, contributed to the overthrow of the idea of the family as cell and norm of society.

We can understand why a grown person can no longer listen, without shuddering or smiling, to the exhortations that Luther addressed to the domestics: "Servants and maidservants should not only obey their masters and mistresses, but more, they should honor them as their own parents. They should do all that is demanded of them, not under compulsion and reluctantly, but with pleasure and with joy, because it is the commandment of God, as we have said earlier, and because this work is more acceptable to him than all the others. Also, far from accepting wages, they themselves ought to pay, too happy for being able to serve their masters, for having a cheerful conscientiousness and for knowing how to make those true works of art which up to now have lost their splendor and have been scorned, while everyone, at the instigation of the devil, hastened to enter the convent, to make pilgrimages, and to buy indulgences." [5]

This text forms part of the commentary on the commandment: "Honor your father and your mother." Following the paternalistic ethic of the age, which indeed saw social organization as an extension or an appendage of family life, Luther extended the validity of this commandment to the servants and maidservants, in short, to all the wage earners of his time. Not only does this system lead to a veritable tyranny in society, where the inferior is delivered over defenseless to the superior, and where authority requires not only that it be obeyed but revered and even loved, but even more it destroys the originality of the family. Being spread over the whole of the social body, the family ceases to be a social formation unique in its genre. This uniqueness is what remains to be defined.

The definition and justification of the family, in its specific character, can be sought only in connection with the meaning of the family for the fulfillment of the human being, of the free person. Now, man cannot be understood as an isolated individual, immersed in a social environment that, like the physical environment, would remain foreign to him or would act on him only by a mechanical pressure or an unverifiable influence. Man is, in himself, social. Sociality is his essential dimension. He becomes himself only in dialogue and encounter in the heart of the community.

However, by the disjointed multiplicity of the relationships in which it engages him, as well as by the overorganization of these same relationships, this essential sociality risks killing all privacy in man, all possibility of self-recovery. When social surroundings and relationships let up for a moment, man finds himself abandoned to a solitude that is for him desolate, tedious, distressing, and destructive of his substance. He is a being who is created for communication with others, created to live in encounter. But he is quickly exhausted and emptied by the *public* character of this communication, by all the artifice that necessarily creeps into it. He is overcome by the very multiplicity of his social functions, which are performed through the use of a multitude of differing roles that he can no longer manage to harmonize. He no longer succeeds in being fully himself in the midst of a social dialectic that his subjectivity renders impossible. He depends on perpetual repressions that become second nature to him.

Thus man has need of finding a place where he can show himself both as a being of communication, dialogue, and sharing and, at the same time, as a private being, that is, as a being who is separate in regard to all his roles and social masks. His subjectivity must be able to manifest itself fully, without, however, degrading itself in individualistic egoism. His liberty must be able to manifest itself without any constraint other than that which comes from love. He has need of knowing in his life a sphere of existence that can be called the *social-private* sphere (this apt expression is again from Jean Lacroix).

This place par excellence is the family, and in the bosom of the family. More particularly still, it is the married couple, i.e., that private society, that nonpublic society, grounded in love, friendship, and companionship, where duality is shown in unity and unity in duality, where, finally, a reciprocity of understanding is established as nowhere else.

Scripture has a sound intuition of the specific character and of the absolute originality of the family, not only in underlining the ontological priority of this institution by placing it before the Fall, but still more in characterizing the meaning of the married couple by these two statements of the Eternal: " It is not good that the man should be alone; I will make a helper fit for him " (Gen. 2:18).

Thus the conjugal family is designed to put an end to the disastrous solitude in which man lived, withdrawn into himself or submerged in an anonymous crowd. It is intended to maintain man in his condition as a being of communication (a being who gives and who receives, and who exists only in this two-way generosity). But at the same time, it is meant to be that society where otherness is reduced to its minimum. Man will have there only one sole partner and one sole witness, his wife, helper, or collaborator, who is like him, by no means through a simple external similitude, but like him in the sense that he is himself like God, i.e., in an analogous fashion. This similitude is so deep that there is a common origin of man and woman. They are separated only in the heart of a preliminary unity: God created man "male and female," says the first account of Genesis (ch. 1:27). And the second account takes up the same idea under a slightly different symbol, that of the creation of woman from the rib of man. This creates astonishment and wonder in the man. He finds in front of him a likeness of himself. It is a fellow being who is, nevertheless, other than himself: " Then the man said ,' This at last is bone of my bones and flesh of my flesh; she shall be called Woman, because she was taken out of Man ' " (Gen. 2:23).

Does not this artless astonishment occur again each time when man encounters, discovers, his helpmate, and when he has the feeling of receiving her? It seems that here the notions of selfishness and of otherness are surmounted without being destroyed. Each one remains capable of personal behavior and decision (which is seen magnificently in the account of the Fall). Each one remains a person, but a person coresponsible with the other, which Adam pretended to forget. Each one remains individual, but in unity with the partner: they have became one sole flesh (ch. 2:24), although they have, being *become* one sole flesh, a different past, different characteristics, different functions.

This existence in unity of two distinct selves must not create between them that secret and pernicious dialectic in which one seeks to baffle the other, that is, to play a role with respect to the other. This is what Scripture, with the realistic symbolism customary to it, emphasizes in saying: " And the man and his wife were naked, and were not ashamed " (Gen. 2:25). Shame is born precisely of the feeling that the individual should hide himself, that he cannot appear before the other as he is, that he must play a part before the other, that the other is no longer his fellow being, but an audience. This attitude is exhausting and ruinous to the personality itself, for perpetually playing a role leads to the point where finally the individual no longer knows who he is. He loses his own intimacy. In the conjugal community, by reason of the similarity of the two partners, by reason of their union in the flesh, the one's real life is presented to the other and, so to speak, dedicated to the other, who is the permanent witness to it. It is only when the witness is transformed into the judge that the conjugal community becomes unbearable.

In short, man escapes from bondages, from lassitude, from the exhausting and partially artificial character of social relationships, through the family and especially through the life of the married couple. Yet he is not for that reason bent back toward that boring solitude in which the self falls in love with itself. The self is not thrown back toward the depressing meditation of suffering, of growing old, and of death, where there is no hope of being able to be freed from anxiety through the sharing and through the acceptance of the anxiety of others.

The family, then, does not bring us out of the community sphere. It does not cut man off from his social dimension. On the contrary, it gives him the possibility of encountering others in his irrepressible singularity. But at the same time it prohibits him from vanishing away in

the general: one's wife is not wife-in-general, constituting
an entire social category. Far from being overcome by
the conjugal community, privacy finds itself best defended
there. For the family forms a sure sanctuary against the
social. It is the place where politics, business affairs, and
civilization do not penetrate without losing something of
their violence or their noxiousness, for the normal family
creates passions capable of barring the way to political
and social passions. In all ages, one sees the family building, with more or less success, a fragile but valuable network to defend itself against the intrusions of public life.
It is always the mark of a profound moral and social crisis
when the political community of interests curtails all family solidarity, and when the law no longer considers the
family tie as superior to every other tie.[6]

Moreover, this absolute singularity of the family is
pointed out by Scripture. The Biblical prerogative of the
family is that it is the only social institution that belongs
to what can be called the Order of Creation. Its founding
is presented to us as uniquely linked to the creative design
of God, whereas all other social forms – in particular, the
political form – are always related to the Fall: cities, nations, kingship, the state, are institutions beneficent for
man on account of sin. Marriage concerns the fulfillment
of his calling, and the family does not have original reference to the Fall. Undoubtedly, with sin it takes a new
meaning and a new function: the apostle Paul clearly indicates this when he emphasizes that it is better, despite
the supposed imminence of the Parousia, to marry than
to burn (I Cor. 7:9). Marriage and the family are barriers
against the outpouring of sin, that is, they participate in
it. Thus we are astonished that Charlotte von Kirschbaum,
so anxious to avoid all natural theology, can write: " All

marriage founded on an authentic and durable love re-
flects something of the original condition of man and
woman before the Fall." [7] Besides, Scripture informs us
that the relationships between husband and wife have
been transformed by the Fall: the authority of the man
increasingly becomes domination, and the woman, carried toward her husband by a *désir-passion,* will be the ac-
complice of the enslaving will of man while at the same
time transferring this will to her own advantage (Gen.
3:16b).

But the family, corrupted by sin, nevertheless preserves
its first meaning, and Scripture can express the authentic
relationships that ought to unite men to God and men
among themselves in the Kingdom only by means of categories that express family relationships: fatherhood and
brotherhood. Even more, the entire regenerated humanity can be conceived of only on the model of a family.
This is also why something of the intimacy of the family,
of family sharing and of the mutual aid that exists in the
family, should be found in the church. The relationship of
Christ to his church is presented in the New Testament
on the model of the conjugal relationship. And previously
in the Old Testament conjugal symbolism was the idiom
of history, that is, of the relationship of God with his
people.

But exactly because conjugal and family relationships
symbolize the authentic history of man, they are marked
with all the disgraces of the Fall. They do not cease to
oscillate between fidelity and adultery, between the grace
of forgiveness and sin. The marriage of Hosea illuminates
at one and the same time the story of the family and the
story of God and man. [8] There is a family *mystique* that is
in no way Christian. It consists of seeing in the family the

refuge of all purity, a little island of holiness in the midst of a sinful world. Nothing permits us to affirm that the human family will subsist in the Kingdom (Jesus tells us only that in the Kingdom there will no longer be a question of marriage). But the relationships that appear in the family society and that it promotes — fatherhood and brotherhood — have an eschatological future to which other human relationships could not lay claim.

In taking notice of this privileged nature of the family, the order of social-private life, we do not, however, wish to affirm that it alone is capable of giving man an experience of existence at once communal and private. Pagan antiquity, as well as Biblical antiquity, knew other forms of the same experience. The most important, undoubtedly, is *friendship*. It should be added that in pagan antiquity the relationship of friendship outclassed by far, if not all family relationships (the father-son relationship always enjoyed an extraordinary privilege), at least the conjugal relationship. This was true even in the midst of a monogamous civilization. Foreign to all carnal ties, to all consanguinity, the relation of friendship undoubtedly lends itself to all kinds of idealization far better than the family tie. It can be more unselfish. Scripture, also, extols the sweetness of faithful friendship. The book of Proverbs even goes so far as to say, " There is a friend who sticks closer than a brother " (Prov. 18:24).

And yet friendship, with its gratuitousness, its contingency, and its surprises, is somewhat less fundamental than the family relationship. It marks man less profoundly than the conjugal relationship, the father-son relationship, or the relationship of brother to brother. Man designates, qualifies, and to a certain degree, describes himself by his family name. Friendship, without a doubt, is the bearer of certain precious values: loyalty, trust, esteem. But the family, which knows and presupposes these same values, contains them within its limits and sustains them by a relationship of appurtenance. If there is a family being, it is because we fit it together from essential physical, psychological, moral, and spiritual traits.

We are tied to our family by a faithfulness that transcends any freely granted commitment, but that at the same time requires such a commitment. To be sure, this belonging can never be entirely ratified by us through an absolutely free act (no more than we can absolutely ratify our belonging to a homeland, which has been given to us more than we have chosen it). This is true, first of all, because our belonging is rooted in depths that we cannot reach. In the second place, we are quite aware of all that is partial, open to criticism, vulnerable, and ironic in belonging to such a family, which has its prejudices, its narrowness, and its pride.

But at the same time, a person would not wish to renounce this belonging, even if he fell out with the members of his family and pretended to deny them. For to renounce this belonging to a family, to break away from this line, to suppose such a thing possible, would be to cut one's own roots. It is through the medium of a family, and not as a detached individual, that a person is rooted in humanity, whereas the animal is linked with his species without the intermediary of a family. For the animal, the family has the characteristics of contingency and accident. There is no human being who is not engendered, in every sense of the word, and there is no human being whose activities, style of living, and vocation are not marked by this engendering. To be is to have ancestors. "A family, or rather, a lineage," Gabriel Marcel has written, "is the suc-

cession of historical modalities according to which the
human genius assumes individual characteristics to the
point of becoming the singular being that he is." The New
Testament, also, characterizes and recognizes the humanity of Christ by his insertion into a genealogy. And the affirmation found so frequently in the Old Testament, according to which the lineage is the mediator of the divine
curse and the divine blessing, should not be immediately
assumed to be a survival of a mythical mentality.

The tragic thing about the " death of the father " is that
one knows quite well that one cannot get rid of the father,
even in killing him. In one way or another, the father will
survive in the individual. The person's rage against the
father is an impotent reality. This half carnal and half
psychic profundity of the family tie explains at once how
it survives the emotions and the extraordinary power that
it acquires when ties of affection are added to it.

However, what the individual could not accomplish,
civilization can attempt. It can reduce (and sometimes increase) the value of the family tie. And this is one of the
aspects of the misfortune of man in the city of antiquity.
The confusion of the social order with the order of being is
one of the consequences of the weakness of the family. Ancient man sought in friendship precisely that refuge that
the family was not able to offer him. But since he was cut
off from his family roots, it was difficult to succeed in maintaining this friendship on the level of pure fidelity and
pure trust. The deterioration, so general even among the
best, of friendship into pederasty reveals this trouble of
man who knows neither family discipline nor family roots.

The attempt to escape this discipline and this deep-
rootedness is manifest in other forms of civilization. As a
general rule, they are the totalitarian societies that more

readily show a mistrust regarding the family tie. Proceeding to the dissolution of all groups that mediate between man and the society at large (political parties, unions, churches, etc.), they group the family among the social realities to be fought against. Not without lucidity, they justly discern this social-private sphere through which man escapes collectivization and dissolution in the midst of the crowd.[9]

CHAPTER II

The Family Communion

THE PRINCIPAL characteristic of the family is that it is a communion at the same time intentional (always difficult to discover and maintain) and voluntary, and also obligatory, necessary, and juridically ordered. In the family, as in the nation, liberty and necessity appear and are confirmed. I am born in *a* family, and yet this family becomes *my* family. The voluntary and the involuntary intersect and are blended together there.

In order for this community to have possibilities for the future, in order that it not become suffering, hell, or a " hornet's nest," it is clearly necessary that the pivot of the family be the love of a man for a woman, of a woman for a man, that requited love which constitutes the conjugal couple as the basis of the family and, on occasion, as the complete family.

We cannot yet speak of this love, for it can be understood in its specific character only in relation to sexuality. For the moment we will consider it only in its flowering in the bosom of the family. It is necessary that this flowering occur in order that the family become a reality. The most passionate, the most fiery, and the most exclusive love is incapable of assuring the existence of the family, or even of the conjugal community, if it is not developed within a range of feelings less ungovernable than itself, more imbued with reason than itself, more open to the action of faith and even to the action of those humble customs and moral conformities which are of such great value in human life. We will call these feelings affection, trust, fidelity, and even friendship. Their stability often allows them to survive *amour-passion*. But in the normal course of events they are also able to transform it, to console it for the amount of illusion that it near-fatally harbors in its beginnings. They are necessary for the maturity of love. The type of puerility that characterizes *amour-passion* cannot continue to exist just as it is. It will not endure the refutations of experience (my wife is neither the most beautiful nor the most intelligent), the inroads of the aging process, the fits of temper. Moreover, it would isolate the married couple, in cutting off all external communities on which the couple ought to find support: groups of friends, groups of colleagues, religious, political, and cultural communities.

But above all, the childishness of *amour-passion* would no longer permit the parents to devote themselves to their children and, what is more important, to create with them a true community. Certainly, the married couple must guard its specific nature in the bosom of the family. The coming of children must not lead to its dissolution. Too often one has the impression that parents, once past a certain age, live only for their children and no longer for each other. Now, the married couple is the stable element of the family. As it preceded the coming of children, so it must survive their departure. This minute society which is the family comprises different spheres: the married couple, the community of children, the community of parents and children. None of these groups should be sacrificed to the others. In order that a true balance be established among them, it is necessary that the love of the man and woman know an evolution. This does not mean a weakening or even an abatement, but only an attenuation of that which love originally possesses exclusively, indeed cruelly. The existence of the married couple is submitted to a tempo. The short life of a family community has a history, and this history moves from jealous possession to sharing.

Let us remark, however, that this evolution should not necessarily be regretted. The violence of *amour-passion* is necessary in order to provoke the encounter of two beings and to draw forth from them that decision, in reality so little natural, to belong to each other forever. A conjugal community that would begin solely by mutual affection and esteem, that would ignore the violence of Eros, would greatly risk remaining a partnership of reason with a philanthropic aim. Must such a type of union be categorically condemned? Not necessarily. There are occasions when true love is born from what was at first only esteem, but this type of evolution is somewhat rare and perilous.

We can here only make allusion to the requisite conditions for the married couple to become a true communion. We cannot yet indicate how it becomes this effectively. In order to do so, we would need a whole theology of love and marriage. This will be outlined in the second part.

Let us agree on the fact that the conjugal communion can be realized and that it is realized under the form of a *covenant* in which each gives himself to the other, in which each ceases to be independent and transfers (let us not hesitate to use the word) to the profit of the other a profound aspect of his liberty, namely, the liberty of choice, the indefinite possibility of choice, the permanent availability for all solicitation and amorous adventure. As popular language puts it, not without truth, the man who marries is " caught." The conjugal community comes into being at this cost.

The New Testament, to be sure, does not expressly define this community as a covenant. Yet what it says of marriage and of the reciprocal duties of the married pair is understandable only insofar as one sees marriage, conforming to the Jewish notions that were current, truly as a covenant.[10] That which characterizes the marriage covenant is the appearance of a unity that, without destroying the singularity of the persons, is superior to them, is a transcendent value for each of them: the married partners are no longer two, but one, one sole flesh (Matt. 19:5). And this term *sarx* (flesh), equivalent here to *sōma*, clearly indicates a personal unity. It is a new person that is created in the couple, giving evidence by its very existence that the human being is not condemned to absolute solitude. The relations between the spouses remain interpersonal relations, but they are also intrapersonal. The family cannot be classified with other social types because no other society presents to this degree the unification of consciousnesses. The family must be necessarily a society that cannot be coordinated to others.

This limited group which is the conjugal group has a brief enough history facing it, and it is called to assume a difficult task. It will first of all have to achieve its own unity. For this is not a given, but a task. Even when the man and wife come from similar social circles,[11] even when the difference in ages between them is not considerable, even when they have a comparable cultural level, it remains no less true that each of them bears his own past. Each of them has behind him a history, and to human sight these two histories are not complementary. Each of them has his singularity, and it is important that unity be realized without killing this singularity. Moreover, marriage is a union of two profoundly different beings. This differentiation is inscribed in nature.

Let us not forget, however, that civilization does not necessarily extend nature. As society can accentuate the distance separating man and woman, imposing on them a different juridical status, different types of life, multiplying the obstacles to communion between husband and wife (and this even in a monogamous system), so, on the contrary, can society unite the sexes, forcing them to the same activities, to the same culture, the same recreation, the same style of life. Civilization sometimes emphasizes natural differences, and sometimes it de-emphasizes them. We live in an age in which woman is on the way toward gaining legal equality with man as a consequence of her professional and cultural equality. As a result, and this is undoubtedly a positive aspect of the current evolution, woman is tending to become more of an aid to man than in the past, both in the family and outside. She is his counterpart, sharing his toil, his anxieties, but also his diversions and his leisure-time activities, having the same friends that he has.

It is sometimes feared that this evolution is resulting in a loss in the femininity of women. But this fear is especially appropriate precisely at the time when woman is obliged to *fight* for the conquest of her rights in order to make herself recognized as the equal of man. The feminine movements for emancipation have the effect of creating an egalitarian style, of threatening woman in her femininity, of urging her not to accept her feminine state, which appears to her as a mark of inferiority. A parallel attitude has certain grave consequences in the life of the married couple, which no longer accepts the mystery of the covenant, conceives of marriage as a free agreement between equals, and is little inclined to those sacrifices which create a true union. It seems that in our countries of the West we have almost left behind this phase of the crisis, whose acute character was due precisely to the fact that legislation is behind mores and that the defenders of the old order try to engage in delaying actions.[12]

Whatever be the evolution of mores and the egalitarian tendency of civilization, it is essential that man and woman by no means forget that they have been *created* different, that each is called to fulfill a different vocation, and that the difference of sex is an essential characteristic of humanity. To take seriously the account of Genesis is to refuse the constant affirmation of Simone de Beauvoir,[13] according to which the sexual differentiation of the human being does not belong essentially to his existence and cannot be compared to corporeality or to death. Perhaps, from a scientific point of view, the determination of the sexes appears to us to have a contingent enough character. Perhaps their differentiation is less absolute than popular common sense imagines it (let us think of all the changes of sex after surgical intervention). And perhaps feminine components subsist in the psychology of some men and the sources of masculinity in the psychology of some women. Nevertheless, the multiplicity of abnormal cases and of limited cases must not make us lose sight of the existence of the creative design of God that calls men and women to a singular vocation. Moreover, education shows us that one does not, with impunity, bring up a boy as a girl or a girl as a boy. The crisis of puberty indicates how young boys and young girls follow a different evolution.[14]

Given the singularity of individual vocations, it is surely

difficult to mark what is peculiar to man and what to woman. In such an attempt there is always the risk of taking a passing sociological datum as absolute. The generation of 1900 would be greatly astonished to discover all the reputedly masculine careers that are today open to women, without any loss of femininity on the part of women. But it is possible to establish an essential difference between the sexes only in reference to the type of authority that belongs to the man and to the woman, and above all, to the husband and to the wife in the bosom of the family. This is why we will attempt to establish this difference only after having considered what the subordination of woman means according to Scripture. For the moment, let us confine ourselves to the affirmation that the harmony of the couple presupposes respect for diversity and that the Christian duty is to resist all attempts of civilization to reduce woman to a servile condition, to make her a possession of man, and that the Christian duty is also to resist all attempts of civilization to efface the distinction between the sexes. Is not one of the symptoms of periods of great moral disarray the wish to eliminate, in fashions and dress, all difference between men and women?

Resting on so many unyielding differences, the harmony of the married couple will always be a task more than a fact. It must be patiently sought. Sometimes it can be gained despite a very bad beginning. The contrasts of character, which often grow more marked with age, make this harmony difficult (it is not in the very first years of marriage that the greatest number of divorces are to be found). The anxieties created by the material difficulties of life, the temptations of professional relationships, the dissensions provoked by the education of the children, growing old (which does not always have the same rapidity in both partners), all these factors increase the difficulty of achieving this harmony which, in the transports of first love, had been taken for granted.

Indeed, personal originality, that I-don't-know-what which brings me to love a certain being, can, from a superficial view, fade away in the course of life, in favor of generic and hereditary traits: how many men have become alienated from their spouses when it was realized that the wives resembled more and more the mothers-in-law?

Social circumstances naturally have an influence on the stability of homes. In particular, overlong separations between husband and wife (e.g., in the course of wars or when the husband is imprisoned) often have the effect of breaking up the household. This is not at all necessarily because of any infidelity on one side or the other, but quite simply because each of the partners has lived certain experiences that could not be shared with the other and because their singular destinies no longer succeed in coming together again. The conjugal commuity is, in fact, characterized by incessant sharing, by a life where each one bears witness to the other. It is for this reason, moreover, that the polygamic system rarely ends, in actual fact, in an authentic state of marriage. The number of spouses renders sharing impossible. It creates between the husband and certain of his spouses a special relationship from which the others are excluded, unless quite simply the spouses become mere material possessions, witnessing to the opulence of the " husband." [15]

No other community involves such demands, namely, the complete transparency of the partners in regard to each other. As soon as one of the partners is the possessor of a secret that he cannot confess to the other, or at least the existence of which he cannot confess to the other, as soon as he tries to share with a third person the secret that he has not been able to confide to his spouse, the community of the conjugal couple is broken. The existence of the couple becomes increasingly vexed by a series of lies, of compromises, which will not take long to render it artificial or untenable, unless the married couple consents to become an association of interests and thereby loses all its specific nature. Even if this association of interests has in view the good of the children, sincerely sought, which becomes then the only tie between the parents, this association is no longer anything more than a caricature of a home. The parents become incapable of offering their children the possibility of forming an integral part of a community in which they themselves have ceased to live. The undertaking would be paradoxical, for the education of the child consists of integrating him into a community that existed before him, that must be a strength and refuge for him. It is necessary that the child be conscious of this living community, that is to say, a community capable of being renewed.

The point is precisely that the family community dies from not being renewed. Perhaps there has been too much insistence on the stability of the family in a changing world. Perhaps stability is the snare of family life. First love has a pretension of being eternal. It wants to last always, and because of this very pretension, it deteriorates in practice. The conjugal community must, from the very first, admit that it is destined to live a history, that in this history many changes will be brought about. Certain new centers of interest will appear, whether for one of the partners or for both. Some renunciations will be necessary, including things that one had resolved not to relinquish.[16]

It is a question, therefore, of giving positive meaning to these renunciations themselves. When man passes the fifty-year mark he often loses his taste for enterprise. He hesitates in his professional life to embark on new and daring undertakings. Prudence triumphs over audacity. It is important that when this happens, his spouse, often younger than he and whose psychological evolution is not, in any case, the same as his, does not reproach him bitterly for this loss of drive. On the contrary, she should aid him to overcome his weariness and to see that restraint and prudence, when they are not accepted with resignation, can have a creative meaning, that they are able to lead to a new fruitfulness. Conversely, the woman is often more versatile than the man and can adjust herself more easily to the changes of existence, and it is important that the husband not discourage her, that he not take umbrage at her facility for renewal, but find there, on the contrary, the protection against his own skepticism or his disillusionment.[17]

Though it is small, the family society has a personal history that derives from the maturation of personalities and from the aging process. But, on the other hand, this history is not cut off from that of the city, in which the events of the world resound so profoundly. The courage with which the married couple assume this double history unites them in common tasks. Resignation isolates them, one from the other.

CHAPTER **III**

The Meaning
of the Presence of Children

THE PROBLEM of the family community is greater than that of the conjugal community. This is a natural consequence of the normal presence of the child or of children, and, even more, of the presence, over against that of the conjugal community, of a community of children who will react in various ways on the former.

What does the presence of the child mean for the couple? It should be emphasized first of all that the child is the seal, the sign, the *objectivication,* as Hegel would say, of the conjugal communion. This is not to say that the child is necessarily, nor always, the manifestation of the conscious intention that animates this new unity, this new flesh that is the married couple. Procreation is very largely independent of the intention, and sometimes even of the wishes, of the parents. But the child reveals to his parents, he unveils after the event, the depth of their carnal unity. He partakes of both. He is both one and the other, and he is this at the same time. He is their duality surmounted in a new unity. For their joy, but also sometimes against their will, he gives witness to that which is unique in their relationship. Strictly speaking, he is the objective likeness of the conjugal communion. He attests, beyond the experience that either parent had of it, the verity of this union.

The child, consequently, cannot be denied. It is in vain that the parents separate. The evidence of their child will always turn against them, showing that in fact the conjugal relationship could never be totally broken, that the rupture is always an artifice, and that the disavowed unity continues to exist in the very person of the child. The unhappiness of the child of divorced parents takes symbolical value: it signifies, beyond all remarriages and all attempts to "remake one's life," the persistence of the injury inflicted on the conjugal union, which is in itself indestructible.

It is also not rare, inversely, that the parents discover, thanks to the presence of the child, the objective depth of the tie that unites them. Because it is first of all lived in the very depth of being, this unity is, in effect, not always conscious in the partners. They come to think in terms of it only through the child, who becomes thus the mediator of their unity. Objectified in the child, this unity is interiorized and understood. One often sees, also, that the child strengthens or saves the unity of the home and that the absence of the child in the home sometimes makes the problem of married life more difficult.

But if the child is thus the sign, seal, and, in some way, the sacrament of the conjugal communion, does it therefore follow that the child is also the aim of it, that the absence of children deprives the conjugal communion of all meaning? This latter is a point of view frequently accepted and one that very often camouflages the failure of a married existence. The parents transfer on their children all the disappointed hopes in their married life. It is quite true that the child can be for the parents the consolation for their personal failure. But this fact does not prove that the family has meaning only through the child.

Scripture presents the child to us as a blessing attached
to the family. The coming of the child results from a special promise of God. It is a grace that is added to that of
the conjugal communion and that confirms it but that is
not intended to replace it.

In any case, the conjugal communion cannot be reduced
to the level of a means to an end. It has its own meaning
in itself. A man marries his wife because he loves her, not
because she can bear him children. Concern for the child,
a figure long ignored in history [18] (entire civilizations have
been able to be founded on the nonrecognition of, if not
the contempt for, children), an essential and not merely a
valid concern, risks obscuring in our age the worth and
the particular reality of the conjugal communion. It is not
impossible that a certain natalist policy is accompanied by
a devalorization of the conjugal bond. In the Roman Catholic Church it is both a dogma and an established practice
that in the case of serious accident at the moment of birth,
an accident endangering the life of the child or of the
mother, it is proper to sacrifice the mother for the child.
It may be that modern techniques make these cruel alter-
natives theoretical enough, but the doctrinal affirmation
remains, nonetheless. It implies the following idea: the important thing is the transmission of life, the filiation and
continuity of generations; the conjugal communion is second.

Catholic thought undoubtedly taps a Jewish idea in this
respect. The value that Israelites attached to the idea of
posterity is well known. It had for them the importance
that the idea of personal survival would take in other civilizations. But this notion of posterity was bound up for
them with the consciousness of election. The result, but
also the proof and the guarantee, of the covenant made by

God with Abraham was the institution and the maintenance of a posterity without imperfection. All the eschatological beliefs of ancient Israel were connected with the
idea of a maintenance of the elect people. And although
Israel admitted proselytes, it is evident that it is Israel according to the flesh, the real posterity of Abraham, to
whom first of all the divine promise was reserved.

However, this idea of a posterity according to the flesh
has rightly ceased to be valid for the Christian church.
There are no longer either Jews or Greeks. All are called,
reconciled in the spiritual household. God has made one
sole people of two peoples (Eph. 2:11-21). The continuity
of the church is not founded on filiation (God shall call
forth a posterity for Abraham from the very stones), but
uniquely on the promise of God that the powers of death
shall never prevail against the church and its foundation
(Matt. 16:18). Thus in the Christian church the idea of
posterity, although it preserves a meaning, is found demythologized, shorn of its sacredness. It ceases to be a
theological necessity.

Yet there are other forces in the modern age that have
contributed to pushing the child to the forestage of history
and to the making of procreation a duty more sacred than
all others. Certain ideologies, and among them national-
ism, see the absolute duty in the child, in his harmonious
development, in the formation of a disciplined citizen and
effective producer. The family has meaning only if it fulfills this responsibility. Moscow has, in a way, come to
the relief of Rome.

It follows from this that not every policy of eugenism or
of natalism is necessarily favorable to the family, in the
sense that it sees the child not as a person who comes to
enrich the family communion and to renew it, but as a

means of assuring the supremacy of the nation or of the race. Well, the child is also a person and it is in the family community that this person takes form.

Scripture grants a privilege to the bond of filiation. It illuminates the parental bond by the relation of the Father and the Son in the bosom of the Trinity. It recalls that all families of the earth take their name, that is, their reality, from the Trinitarian God and that the family communion can be compared to nothing other than the relationship of the living God with his people. And in doing this, Scripture asks us not to refuse the child the eminent place he ought to have in the heart of the family, but rather to look after the preservation of the family communion. The New Testament presents this communion to us as a reality so decisive that it even attains a spiritual meaning: the faith of a father or of a mother can obtain from Jesus the healing of a child; the children of a Christian couple are declared holy. It is in the houses, i.e., in the families, that the nascent church constitutes itself. It is an entire family that believes and that receives Baptism collectively.

And yet, despite all this, Scripture does not present the family to us as an absolute, at least not in the New Testament. The decision of faith can lead to the breaking of family ties. Jesus puts above his own family those who do the will of God and who are, from this fact, his true parents, brothers, and sisters. And the early church knew that the ecclesia must be able to replace the family community that had been broken by one's having made a decision of faith (Mark 10:28-30).

But outside of these admittedly exceptional cases where a person is called, by divine vocation, to break the family tie, the family is presented to us as the preeminent occasion for insertion into humanity and into the church. It is by filiation much more than by other forms of human solidarity that the unity of human creation is attested. If the Christian name bears witness to the singular vocation of each one, the surname testifies to one's belonging to mankind. The child, considered as a person even before he has reached the independence of adulthood, is thus the first opportunity for the parents to do human work, to participate in the human adventure. It is not without reason that the account of Genesis puts procreation and culture on the same level and sees there two aspects of the same vocation of humanity. Procreation for man, differing from that of animals, is not simply a matter of contributing to the perpetuity of the species. It attests that man believes in the future of humanity, that he knows that there is a future for this humanity. And how could this knowledge be assured apart from faith in the carrying out through history of the design of God? Even now the growth of the birthrate can have the importance of a sign in the midst of a nation. It is evidence that the national community faces its future with confidence, that it is not contracted on its past, that it does not conceive of existence as a contentment with the enjoyment of accumulated goods or in the attainment of comfort, but rather that it is worth the trouble to build a better future. Shortly after the last world war the birthrate in France knew a rise unforeseen and without parallel in the annals of history [19] (the fall in the birthrate had begun as early as the middle of the eighteenth century). This was evidently the result of a will of renewal that permits one to hope that other mortgages will be raised.

But once again this wager on the future, even if it has reasonable motives, even if it flows from a reasoned confidence, remains uncertain as long as one does not perceive that all human history, far from being a succession of events devoid of meaning, moves toward a fulfillment. It is not, therefore, by chance that the Christian churches have always encouraged natality, and have faced only reticently and with qualifications the problem of birth control. They are conscious that man is called to participate in the preservation of the Creation, as well by procreation as by the various activities that are conducive to assuring man's domination over the world. God attaches worth to this preservation because it is the very condition of the unfolding of his redemptive activity, namely, of the activity by which God leads the world to its fullness of creation. It is, in fact, " the theater of his glory " (Calvin). Thus the presence of the child in the family bears witness that God pronounces the yes of his mercy on the projects of men. It is in this sense that the child is truly the blessing of God.

By means of the child, God offers to the human couple the opportunity to go beyond itself. If the couple is one sole flesh, this flesh is going to know all the temptations of egoistic isolation. The presence of the child, whatever be the economic conditions in which the family lives, will mean the acceptance of a sacrifice on the part of the parents. It will mean a sacrifice of their self-sufficiency, of their serenity, a common acceptance of concern for the other, an acceptance of manifold servitudes. Above all, it will mean an acceptance of the risk and of the responsibility for the education that has as its object precisely to insert the child into the human race, to develop in him all the possibilities of humanity.

Consequently, it is valid to look at the child as a surpassing of oneself, and, even more, as the merciful sign come from God, so that death itself does not constitute the absolute catastrophe, does not constitute the end of one-self. Each person lives on, and the married couple lives on in its children. This conviction is expressed not only in the immemorial practice of bequeathing something to one's children but in the desire (sustained, moreover, by nature) to give something of oneself to one's children, even if it is only an ambition, only a conviction, a manner of living in the world and of taking the world upon oneself. There is no one who, in terms of his life, can say to himself, "Well done, good and faithful servant." Even so-called "natural" death, coming at the time when a man is full of years, always signifies a failure, a break. To man, subjected to the hard law of death, God offers the possibility, thanks to the child, of handing on something of himself in his progeny. And it is permitted to man, even to the Christian, to adopt once again, in considering his children, the pagan formula: *Non omnis moriar*.[20] In fact, the progressive despoilment that growing old signifies, and that total despoilment which is death, is made easier for man, to whom the grace is given to live on in his children.

Although we have dismissed the theological meaning that Israel attached to lineage, we can here recover one meaning. God knows how much, in the present economy, death remains the enemy of man. By entrusting to him the care of children (whether this is by procreation or by adoption), it makes death easier for him and prevents him from quitting this life in bitter resignation ("After me the deluge"). It would be quite normal, accordingly, for all the families on earth to organize an outraged and active protest against all human enterprises that encumber or endanger the future of our children, against all forms of genocide, against the thoughtless use, for military ends, of atomic energy.

Naturally, it is necessary that parents know how to show versatility and imagination when they think of living on in their children. On the one hand, it is not sufficient, and often not desirable, for one to live on in his children by certain traits of character. On the other hand, the bourgeois civilization of the West, of which we are the inheritors, has long persuaded us that it is essential to bequeath to our children, with no consideration given to their own inclinations, a certain professional orientation, the management of an enterprise. It is evident that we do not have the right to load the generations that follow us with unjustified burdens. This is all the more true since we will bequeath to them, whether they want it or not, a hereditary burden that they would be able to do without. We must take care not to be excessive testators. Precisely because our children must be the agents in God's hands of a certain fulfillment of history, and — why not? — of a certain progress, it is necessary for us to consider them with respect and to bequeath them less a capital, with its enslavements, than certain tasks, great tasks to accomplish, those tasks of which we ourselves have been shown unworthy. It is possible that in certain periods of history the only thing that one will be able to bequeath to his son is the balance sheet of a failure. But this balance sheet can itself be of considerable worth. It is not fruitless to be able to write, as Leon Blum did in his last book: " The generation to which I belong has not been successful in its task. I know it as well as anyone, but I do not rise to present its defense. Of its faults, of its illusions, of its unhappiness I try to draw some lesson for the generations that follow, for those who will carry the responsibility tomorrow." [21] Our experience can profit others more than ourselves.

If there is, in this type of thinking, a collective duty of

each generation toward that which follows it, all the more reason does the individual have to render account to his own children. But this act of humility, which is at the same time a surpassing of the self, will take complete worth only if it is not solely the act of the individual, but the act of the married couple in the midst of which each partner will have performed the most authentic adventure of his existence.

Do these considerations mean that a family without children, which has not been able or has not wished to take the risk of adoption, should consider itself as an incomplete family? Assuredly not. There is such a profound unity in the conjugal community that it should be able to do without the child. It should not want to do without it, for this would be presumption on its part and scorn regarding the promise of God. If the question of the voluntary limitation of children is to be a problem, it is from this point of view that it will be necessary to deal with it, to ask the parents if they truly have a serious reason for refusing a possibility that is objectively offered to them. But in no case should the absence of children be felt to be a failure by the married couple, since their communion has a full and sufficient meaning by itself. Through their communion it is given to them to move beyond their egoistic solitude and to know the joys and the hardships of a shared existence.

Moreover, it will be necessary to emphasize the positive meaning of this absence of children: God calls certain couples to live in a perfect communion without the support and without the visible symbol of children. Such a couple should ask itself if there is not in this the indication of a special vocation, if it is not called to fulfill a special task that the presence of children would hinder or

make impossible. The absence of children creates an availability that can be creative. Parents without children become aware of this easily enough. But it is not sufficient
simply that each of them accepts on his side often very
heavy responsibilities. The decisive thing for such a couple is that it take care to do a common work, that it devote
itself to that which gives the couple the sign of its unity
in a common work. The solidarity established by Scripture between procreation and culture must in this instance be confirmed. It is important that the conjugal
unity be able to be reflected in a mirror of itself. This
common work is not always offered as a possibility by the
world.

The church, also, must be particularly attentive to childless couples. It should not leave them on the periphery of
church life, but should ask them to accept a special ministry in the church. It is, certainly, quite evident that this
same requirement is valid for the household filled with
children. But in this case there is less urgency about it,
because in any event the presence of children and the
problems of their education offer the partners a common
task. The accomplishment of this common task will coun-
terbalance the professional necessity in which each partner accomplishes his own particular work that does not
necessarily create points of contact between them.

The presence of the child and of children will pose new
problems for the home, for which a ready-made solution
does not exist and for which it is necessary to take into
account the personality of each child. Let it suffice for the
moment to enumerate them. First, there are the problems
of education. It should be added that education never consists solely of submitting a child to a discipline, of
strengthening him in his dependence. Rather, it is exactly

to make a free being of him, a being who can get by without his parents, as well as to see that this approach to independence is accomplished without a breach.

Secondly, there are the problems (a special aspect of the preceding ones) of the integration of the child into the family community, that is, the transformation of the natural dependence of the child regarding his family into a tie of association. The procedures here are quite diverse. Let us point out only that the traditional method in France of including the children at an early age in that aspect of family life which the meals constitute is a good method, even if it deprives the parents of their peace and quiet. This should not be curtailed, if possible, even when there are guests. For it is exactly through the conversation of adults that the child is integrated into social life. For the same reason, it is good that the practice has disappeared, which was constant in the French family of preceding generations, of imposing on the children strict silence at the table. It is good for the child to let his parents know of his experiences and of his problems. It is good for him to receive through his parents the echo of the most diverse social preoccupations.

Of course, prudence will be essential on the part of the parents. Married life has its secrets, which are not necessarily those of sexual intimacy, but which can also be material or spiritual concerns that the parents have. They have a duty to keep these concerns from their children, for children are prone to let such concerns obsess them quite acutely and depressively.

In any case, the integration of the child into the family community is a delicate matter. The breaking of the natural tie between the child and his parents may, indeed, come about quite by itself and develop, not always without accident, it is true, from the breaking of the umbilical cord and the weaning process, right up to the formation of a personal intimacy. But the voluntary integration of the child into the family community is not always achieved automatically. Very often it happens that the child falls back toward his solitude or that his personality is smothered by the pressures of the family group.

The child's integration into the family group is aided by his participation in the group of his brothers and sisters, in the sibling community. This community has the value for him of being based on a certain equality. The older children, in any event, provide models for the younger ones by reason of their greater independence and of their *savoir-faire*. It can be a model for the better or for the worse. Yet normally it is the better that prevails. One can see today that in certain large housing developments where only young married couples live, and where there are consequently only very small children, the deficiency in the number of older children makes itself sharply felt. The psychological and moral evolution of the younger children takes place less easily when they are not guided, induced, or restrained by older children. The sibling community sets them free from the stifling aspects of parental authority, even if this authority is loving in intention and is only the authority of prestige.

Paradoxically, it is necessary that the child know a certain detachment with regard to his parents in order that he can form a society with them. The school and the society of comrades provide, certainly, this detachment. But the integration of the child into the school group is made more easily through the mediation of the sibling community. It is only when the child has been brought to assume certain responsibilities in the midst of the sibling community, when he has been associated with the family life as a person and no longer as an object of affection or an object of concern — or an object of reprimand — that he becomes a social being.

It is certain that the sibling community participates with the parents in the education of the children. It is not even exaggeration to say that it educates the parents themselves in certain circumstances and on certain points, in making them attentive to the evolutionary nature of the family. Where the single child is incapable of making his parents understand that he has grown up, the sibling community has more success. In other respects, it constitutes a natural cell of coeducation of the sexes that will have value later in facilitating and making more natural the relationships between young boys and young girls on the outside of the family.

In order for it to play these various roles, which it usually fills spontaneously and unconsciously, it is necessary for the sibling community to meet certain conditions. It must present a certain homogeneity, that is to say, the differences of ages among the children should not be too considerable. Naturally, for very large families this cannot be the case. But then the oldest children can detach themselves from the sibling community, easily and usefully becoming coeducators with the parents. It is important, nevertheless, that the parents do not charge the older children prematurely and too heavily with responsibilities. This is what too often happens in families where the mother is absent from the home.

The attention of psychologists has been directed lately at the necessity of the child's participation in an egalitarian society, for the sake of his moral development and his integration into the social group. As the school group, in the case of children from six to eleven years, develops around the personality of the teacher, so it is important for the child — and, for even greater reason, for the adolescent — to know nonschool groups in which he can manifest his opinion and his aggressiveness without fear, groups in which the adult personality is absent. The sibling community is the first group that responds to this need. It ought to be continued in the different evolutions of youth.[22]

Is there a family optimum? In order for the sibling community to be able to play its role, but also in order for the parents to exercise their parental functions intelligently, the number of children should not be too high. The disappearance, or at least the considerable decline, in most of the countries of Western Europe and of America, of large families with twelve or fifteen children assuredly constitutes a true good.[23] The reduction in the number of children is a sociological phenomenon that advantageously affects all modern countries. It is easy to understand this phenomenon. " As long as the father of the family," writes A. Sauvy, " made use of an absolute authority, as long as he made his children work and as long as a great capriciousness of conditions was tolerated on the interior of the family (children left without care, picking and stealing a miserable nourishment outside), economic interest was in a large family. . . . Children reared in this way died in large numbers, but those who lived produced for their parents from the time they were of the age to work, i.e., from eight to ten years, perhaps before." [24] The intervention of public power, which progressively limited and finally completely prohibited child labor, created on the other hand the obligation of schooling and increased the legal responsiblity of parents. This made children burden-

some, and undoubtedly also precious. The decline in the
rate of infant mortality enhanced the moral worth of the
child. Montaigne was an exception to this, not knowing
how many children he had had.

By a sort of fatalistic acceptance, humanity long admitted that it was natural to lose children. Consequently, the
emotional concern rested, in the main, on children, on
their number rather than on the individual person of the
child. We can see that it is still this way in many underdeveloped countries. The child has become an individual
only when he has passed the threshold of infant mortality. The singular absence of the child in the classic literature of the West up until the nineteenth century is a particularly significant sign of the nonrecognition of the child
as a person.

Juridically, the rights of the child appeared only with
the progress of hygiene and medicine and the spontaneous
reduction in the number of children. The extremely high
birthrate of the countries of the Far East, of the Middle
East, and of North Africa corresponds to a very exagger-
ated infant mortality rate and also to a necessary nonrecognition of the rights of the child. It is proper to recall in
this connection that humanity discovers essential moral
values often only after certain sociological conditions are
achieved.

In the conditions that are ours in the Western world,
can one determine a family optimum? The determination
of this optimum depends on multiple economic and social
factors, of the sort that it will vary according to the social
classes (the incidence of family income and of housing
conditions). In a very judicious article, one free from dog-
matism, R. Debré [25] placed this optimum between three
and six children. It is not difficult to guess the reason for

this. With less than three children there is not really a sibling community, that is, a community of children where temperamental differences can neutralize themselves instead of juxtaposing themselves. With more than six children it is difficult for the parents, one at least of whom devotes the greatest part of his time to his professional life, to give them an individualized and individualizing attention and affection, to prevent certain of the children from being or believing themselves to be rejected to the periphery of the family.

CHAPTER IV

The Problem
of Authority in the Family

B ECAUSE the family is a community, and even a double community, it knows a problem of authority.
Now, the problem of authority is one of the most difficult
of social problems, and it is one that modern societies resolve very poorly. It is not that a social group can never
exist without authority, but that the very exercise of authority usually engenders two opposite, symmetrical, and
sometimes contemporaneous evils. On the one hand, there
is conformity, the blind submission that is a sign of the
degradation of the person as the center of initiative and
choice. On the other hand, there is revolt, the personalist
virtue of which is doubtless greater, but which frequently
develops on its own, engendering nihilism and terror and
impairing all social relationships. The public unrest found
in many of our modern societies is evidence of their incapacity to establish and to recognize an authority that acts
in favor of the community of persons. Either it alienates
persons, or it abandons them to the violence of their revolt.

This situation is reflected in that small society which is
the family, the mirror of the society at large. The family
has been a very authoritarian society. To the extent that
the community character of the family is affirmed it tends

to become less authoritarian. But then the authority of the family becomes very unsteady. In fact, the present-day family is sometimes the place where the abdication of authority is most clearly recorded.

And yet the privileged nature of the family appears in the fact that the problem of authority should be less difficult there than in other social groups. First of all, in the conjugal family, scaled down to include the parents and minor children, authority is exercised effectively over the minors, who know themselves and feel themselves to be minors, despite their sporadic inclinations toward independence. They have need of a protection that guards them against both external dangers and against the immoderate supplications of their own whims and desires. In many cases the child is quite happy to be guarded by paternal protection.

In the second place, this authority is not exercised *ex abrupto;* it is exercised with the support of ties of concrete dependence, on the instinctive and carnal ties to which ties of affection are added, or rather, which become conscious under the forms of ties of affection. Also, paternal authority can, in the majority of cases, be effective without appearing as authority and without recourse to methods of restraint.

In the third place, paternal authority is almost obscured by the prestige that surrounds the figure of the parents in the eyes of the child, a prestige that he himself protects and defends against the disappointments of experience. We can give to this term of prestige all its religious and mythical signification. The parent retains this prestige from the fact that he responds to the helpless desires of the child by his inexplicable acts of power, from the fact that he magically produces what the child desires. He possesses a force and a skill of which the child cannot perceive the limits or the fact that they have been acquired naturally, but which he sees ordinarily operating in his favor.

Finally, this authority is exercised not by means of abstract orders, not by means of applying an inner rule, but in a personal relationship with the child. This permits it to be explained, to be justified, to be qualified in various ways, to be accepted in the measure that the child is capable of sensing the intention of it.

This is why it is, or can be, a limited authority. It can see the consequences of what it decrees. It is able to correct itself in the course of the execution of the orders it gives, adjusting itself to the reactions of the child and molding itself according to the intuitive knowledge that the parents have of the child. Without doubt, this authority is not safe from perversions (there are cases, particularly frequent among very young parents, where the parents are brutal to their children, where they torture the children). Nor is there any doubt that it is not safe from the outbursts of passion, anger, and impatience. But since in our age it is only very rarely a question of monarchical authority, but, rather, of a shared authority, such fits of anger cannot hold out very long against the silent protest or against the looks of disapproval from the other partner. The violent clashes between parents and children and the failures and impotent exasperation of paternal authority take on a dramatic character only at the age of the crisis of juvenile originality. This is, of course, precisely the time when paternal authority should not disappear, but should modify its nature in order to make a place for free discussion. This is the time when the personal behavior of the parents, their wisdom, and their dignity ought to make an impression on the children.

All these reasons explain why authority and obedience should normally be experienced in the family. No social group could validly take the place of the family, for outside of the family it is always the abstract and impersonal authority of a system, or the tyrannical authority of a false personalism, or finally, simple comradeship that prevails. This is why, even though the family is not the social cell and is not extended into the society at large, it is nonetheless a condition of existence for all of society. It gives society men who know the value of authority and of obedience, and the value of the dialectic between them.

Also, we should note that Scripture, in the Old as in the New Testament, reserves the rights of paternal authority with an insistence that is not solely the result of a patriarchal society. It exhorts children to render obedience and honor to their parents. Now, in the body of the Old Testament at least, the family where this authority is exercised does not have absolute meaning in itself. Its meaning is to assure filiation, the lineage that guarantees the perennity of the people of God throughout history. The obedience and honor rendered to parents goes to those who transmit the divine law and who, in transmitting the law and circumcising their children, integrate them into the covenant concluded between God and his people. The parents possess an authority, known to have been harsh and strict, as initiators to this existence in the heart of the people of the promise. The meaning of the family and of parental authority appears clearly in the Old Testament as the initiation and introduction to the life of a community more comprehensive and more critical than the family.

The New Testament, being more sensitive to the personal vocation of each in the midst of the community of the church, increasingly and unobtrusively accentuated that which moderates parental authority. This authority is exercised over a person, over those children whom the Lord wants to receive the same position as adults. It must, therefore, recognize this person even in his capacity for revolt. This is the source of the double exhortation of the Letter to the Colossians: " Children, obey your parents in everything, for this pleases the Lord. Fathers, do not provoke your children, lest they become discouraged " (ch. 3:20-21). The apostle sees clearly that this paternal authority, based on the tie of blood and on a millennial tradition, can produce an exasperation in the child that will lead him, if not to rebellion, at least to a dejected giving up. It is no less significant that in his letters the apostle addresses himself directly to the children, as to authentic addressees placed on the same rank as the adults. The child is a fair way toward becoming a person.

But who will exercise this authority? In the view of our present-day Western civilization there is no doubt about the answer: the parents, jointly and severally. Each one, undoubtedly, will exercise it in his manner, following the particular bent of his sex. The father will have more objectivity, being aware of the educative end to attain. There will be more continuity and sometimes more severity in his exercise of authority. The mother, on the other hand, will give sharper attention to the concrete situation of the child, to the difficulties that truly try him, to his extent of fatigue and of nervousness. But she will often have less concern than the father for the end of education — to bring the child to a state of majority — for she accepts less easily than the father the idea that the child leaves infancy and becomes independent of her. The progressive emancipation of the child represents a series of

crises for her that repeat those of birth, of weaning, and
of the first departure for school. Thus she will often be
less steadfast in maintaining the decision made. Yet it is
necessary to take account of the fact that these traits of
temperament are not attached to the sex in an absolute
fashion and that the situation to which we make allusion
is often reversed.

The fact remains that the recent emancipation of
woman has placed her on an equal footing with man in
the exercising of parental authority. Does it follow that
the problem is resolved? Does the problem not continue
to exist in the very interior of the conjugal community?
Who, in the interior of the couple, will exercise authority?
In fact, this problem is far from being resolved. The consequence is that parents are incapable of exercising, jointly
and severally, authority in the bosom of the family. Fric-
tions and conflicts result from it, of which the child is the
victim, unless he is the mischievous beneficiary of it.

Thus we are placed before this serious question of authority between husbands and wives. The question has received a traditional answer in the Christian West. This solution, presented to us as directly inspired by Scripture,
confirms the superiority of man and the woman's duty of
submission. This traditional solution, at the present time,
is called into question by the evolution of mores. The juridical obligations of civil marriage already give evidence
of a very clear retreat from the obligations embodied in
the marriage liturgies of the Christian churches.

Let us recognize, first of all, that the letter of Scripture
does indeed seem to authorize the conception that radically subordinates woman to her husband. On the one
hand, the account of Genesis clearly records a priority to
man, a chronological priority that symbolizes an ethical
priority. The woman is created after him and for him, so

that he can have at his disposal an aide similar to himself. The second account of Genesis accentuates more the physical dependence, since there the woman appears created from man. The account of the Fall once again confirms this position of inferiority: if woman proceeds with her desire toward man, he dominates over her. Certainly, it is indeed a question here of a penalty, but after all, we have not yet left the economy of sin.

Let us add that the Old Testament shows woman, in effect, as a kind of property of man, a precious property doubtless, but this fact does not affect the dignity of the woman any less. She is a being always under guardianship. Before her marriage she is under the dominance of her father (I Sam. 18:17), and then she passes under the tutelage of her husband, and if he dies, she falls under the authority of the oldest son. She enjoys consideration only as the mother of the children that she has given to the family. Certainly, one could qualify in certain ways the background of this juridical setting, which was valid for the Oriental world as a whole. It is striking, in fact, that woman fulfilled certain religious functions, including duties in the sanctuary (Ex. 38:8), participating in religious festivals (Deut. 12:12; II Sam. 6:19), sacred dances (Judg. 21:21) and sacrificial meals (II Sam. 6:19). Certain women, prophetesses or judges, were able to play an eminent role in the life of the people. All these facts witness that in certain epochs at least, and not the latest ones, the stranglehold that held the woman in tutelage loosened. The Old Testament tradition, in any case, is not absolutely homogeneous. The texts of Genesis, despite the evident priority they give to man, take pains to raise woman to the level of man: a helper similar to him, a being who comes to put an end to his solitude.

What is more, the question can be asked, Do the texts

describing the juridical status of woman have the same theological weight and, consequently, normative value as those texts which announce an anthropological verity on the situation of woman? Are the former limited to making allusion to facts of civilization, whereas the latter would show us that, despite these facts of civilization, in spite of the humiliating juridical situation of woman, the woman as creature of God was recognized in her own being?

However, we should not neglect to say that the New Testament does not consider calling into question this juridical status of woman. It does not condemn the institutions made by and for man, but, rather, seems to bring to them a sort of ratification in repeating insistently that woman ought to be subjected to her husband. Undoubtedly, it settles at the same time the man's fundamental duties toward his wife, and the content of these duties attests that the wife is a person and not a thing: "Wives, be subject to your husbands, as is fitting in the Lord. Husbands, love your wives, and do not be harsh with them" (Col. 3:18-19). The order of submission that is given to woman has priority here, and is not obviated by the fact that the wife is to be the object of love.

There can be no doubt that Christianity has long understood the New Testament laws of submission in a conservative sense, as the guarantee of a social order founded on the power of the man. Also, a reactionary movement has figured vis-à-vis all the democratic, egalitarian movements of emancipation. Even at the present time the Christian churches, greatly divided in other respects, band together at least in order to forbid women access to any function of authority and even to any ecclesiastical function,[26] a situation intended to underline the lesser dignity of woman (we do not always admit it). Have not certain

Norwegian bishops gone so far as to declare that the ordination of women pastors would constitute a malediction for the church and for the interested parties themselves, as well as for the persons who would have recourse to their ministry?

However, the conservative conclusions that Christianity has drawn from a rather abstract reading of Scripture do not exhaust the question. We do not think that it is possible to speak abstractly and absolutely concerning the command of obedience given to woman, as if this command were given to partners completely alien to each other, one of whom should yield to the other. The command is valid and becomes meaningful only in the context of a previous unity, only in the bosom of conjugal unity.

It is incontestable that in the testimony of Scripture man is created chronologically first and that the apostle Paul did not hesitate to make use of this fact in order to bring out the superiority of man and to emphasize man's authority over woman: "For man was not made from woman, but woman from man" (I Cor. 11:8-9). However, this reference to the second account of Genesis must not make us forget the invaluable indications of the first, where it appears that the true human unity created at the very first by God is man and woman: "So God created man in his own image, in the image of God he created him; male and female he created them" (Gen. 1:27). It is not sexual bipolarity that constitutes the image of God in man. The image of God consists, rather, in this unity of the human person, but this unity overlays sexual bipolarity. Woman does not intervene as an instrument, as an accessory designed to furnish the world of man and to make his existence agreeable. Woman is essential to man as man is essential to woman. Creation would not be human without this duality and this unity, without this duality of persons in the unity of the couple.[27]

If we look at the second account more closely, we will see that it says the same thing. The creation of woman from man bears evidence of their personal unity. God himself states the reasons for the creation of woman: " It is not good that man should be alone; I will make him a helper fit for him " (Gen. 2:18). Is this not to say that human existence has no meaning for man alone? Does it not mean that human life makes sense only in community with a being both similar and different, with a partner who is not simply the reflection of man, but who can be both united with him and contrary to him? Let us not arbitrarily reduce, following the variations of our present-day meanings of words and of our economic and utilitarian perception of things, the meaning of the term " helper." The helper in this context is not a hired hand. God himself presents the woman to the man, and the man acclaims her as an exceptional being. In a sort of wonder, he distinguishes her clearly from other creatures: " This at last is bone of my bones and flesh of my flesh " (Gen. 2:23). He recognizes her as a human being, and what is more, he recognizes himself in her. And immediately after this recognition (ignoring the external logic of the account, but with a profound coherence), God emphasizes that man is fulfilled in his wife, in the sense that he becomes truly *adult* through her: " Therefore a man leaves his father and his mother [a symbol of the passage to adulthood] and cleaves to his wife [to cleave is not to possess, the word indicating here a relationship of interpersonal fidelity], and they become one flesh " (v. 24). The fulfillment is in this appearance of one flesh. One could not underline more clearly the equal ontological dignity of man and woman, called to constitute together the human unity upon which the blessing of God rests.

It would be erroneous to believe that the analogy between God and man resides essentially and uniquely in the fact of human duality. It resides also in the power of domination given to man. Nevertheless, it is not accidental that the two notions of the image of God and of the duality of man are found juxtaposed in Gen. 1:27. Although the communion of the couple does not, of itself, constitute the image of God, it reminds us that God himself is not a solitary essence either, and that he has not wished that man be a solitary being. The term " image " should not, obviously, be taken in the precise sense of " type " or " archetype." This has sometimes been done, and has led to the establishing of a term-for-term correlation between man and God, between woman and the Son, between conjugal love and the Holy Spirit. Yet it seems legitimate to us to affirm that the reference to the community life of God, to the reality of the Trinity, which is implied by the notion of the image of God (the human couple being this image), assures us that there is indeed a fundamental equality between man and woman.

Karl Barth has expressed this clearly in a passage [28] that can be summarized, following Fr. Bouillard, in this way: " Man is for woman, and woman for man, the other preeminently, the *Mitmensch*, with whom the exchange of glance, of word and of assistance constitute the need, the problem and the fulfillment in the highest degree; so much so that all relationship between man and man, between woman and woman, appears only as a prelude or an accompaniment to this essential encounter. There, indeed, the contrasts are so strong and the attraction so imperative that the encounter presents the maximum both

of difficulty and of interest. It is not solely a question of
the amatory and matrimonial relationship. But it is clear
that in this relationship the encounter of man and woman
attains its own character and its fullness. It is there that
the free opening of the heart to the other assumes its most
natural and strongest form. Whoever would know nothing
of this domain would also know nothing of the I and Thou
that constitute humanity. One can wonder which is the
most characteristic trait of Nietzsche, the prophet of solitary humanity: his refusal of Christianity or his contempt
for women. The two are necessarily linked." [29] Man and
woman, the image of God in their person-to-person relationship, could not be understood as two beings tied solely
by a hierarchical bond.

In any case, the account in Genesis shows us quite
clearly that woman has the same liberty as man, the same
power of initiative, the power to convince her husband
through the word. This is seen in the account of the Fall,
where Eve serves as mediator between her husband and
the tempter. Interrogated by God about his offense, Adam
shifts the responsibility for it onto his wife, thus unwit-
tingly acknowledging a full dignity to her. He styles her
as flesh of his flesh, as person and partner. He wants to see
her as a stranger, for whom he no longer feels responsible.
Until the rupture, man and woman appeared as persons.
And what is produced here between man and woman is re-
produced in each rupture between humans. The break
consists always in the refusal to be responsible for the
other (Cain will say: " Am I my brother's keeper? ") and
in the desire to assume responsibility only for oneself, as
a distinct being.

Still, this rupture between man and woman does not
bring about a separation. As man, after the sin, did not

lose his function of domination over the world, no more can he be separated from his wife. God destroys nothing of what he has created. But the relationship between man and woman, which continues to exist, assumes another face. They know shame before each other, and God, in giving them clothing himself, ratifies the new situation, if not as good, at least as necessary. This is an invaluable ethical indication; the moral life establishes its norms and its ideals (modesty is manifestly a moral ideal) in the time of sin and in reference to sin. The ethical life does not consist of an impossible angelism. Whoever wishes to play the angel — in the economy of sin — plays the fool. Moreover, and in relation to this shame that expresses both the reserve and the dignity of each creature, but at the same time the transparency between beings, the relationships between man and woman are, moreover, no longer free and reciprocal attachment, free and reciprocal love; they become relationships of domination on the part of man, of desire on the part of woman (Gen. 3:16). A certain passivity appears thus inherent in the situation of woman; she offers herself to man, but there is also a trap, an inveiglement, in this passivity. Man takes her and dominates her, but there is also desire in this domination. It should be remarked that this new situation is not a curse on the part of God. Only the serpent is cursed; men are punished. But this punishment is still for their good. It makes their new condition acceptable, noncatastrophic: " Free love is now subjected to the limits that nature and history impose: violence, threats, and suffering. Man *must* work and woman *must* suffer, man must be responsible for woman and woman must feel desire for man and abide by his will. Whether they want it or not, each is limited to the other, each is committed to the other. Marriage becomes a *conjugium,* a yoke imposed on the despotism of eroticism, a community of work; in place of a pure and joyful satisfaction, it becomes a juridical order imposed on violence and depravity." [30]

This authority of man over woman, this primacy of masculine initiative, does not at all imply the slavery of woman. It does not deliver woman over to the arbitrariness of man. It does not diminish the considerable power that woman has, the power of seduction (in every sense of the word). It is in this sinful condition, within this juridical and nonmetaphysical bond, that man must love his wife and protect her. In effect, his authority determines a juridical order. Man is the head of woman in order that the excess inherent in sin can be checked by established authority, in order that there be some recourse in the case of conflicts: such is, actually, the meaning of authority.

But authority is also exercised on whoever possesses it. At the very moment where the apostle Paul calls this order and this situation to mind (I Cor., ch. 11), he hastens to add that woman is the glory of man, *doxa* (v. 7). And this usage of the term means not only adornment, an object in which man can take pride in the eyes of his fellowmen. It has all its noble meaning here. It is the term that the New Testament employs to designate the appearance of God in history, his incarnation itself: the Son is the glory of the Father. Now, although the Son comes after the Father and is begotten of him, there is equality between the Father and the Son. The glory of man that is woman gives, then, a dignity to woman that cannot be lost. [31]

This affirmation of principle, this guarantee of order that the authority of the husband represents, precisely because it constitutes a limit to the outbreak of the common sin of man and woman, can be understood and embodied according to various modalities, in various ages of history and following various levels of culture and civilization. It is interesting to see how a modern philosopher, Alain, in considering the thought of Auguste Comte, has been able to understand and justify this authority of man and this type of subordination of woman. The authority of man, according to Alain, is expressed and justified in the fact that it is the mediator and agent of physical necessity, of the natural and social order. It expresses the order of the world from which one cannot escape at any price. It submits itself and submits its own, " so great is the source of the commandment; for it is not man who commands; it is the thing, the real and present situation. The government of the male resembles all government; its decrees are always founded on a state of fact that is not at all concerned about whether or not it pleases. It is necessary here to clear away much and to tear down much. After the natural function of sex, which is the Herculean function, its role is to announce the presence of external necessities and to put an end to pleasant reveries. When woman escapes from masculine domination, she immediately finds herself in the presence of the forces of reality. She has only changed masters." [32] It is interesting to note that Alain, as does Scripture, links the authority of man to work, that is, to the battle with external necessity, natural or social.

Feminine thought and ethics, on the contrary, are primarily tied to the actions that complete woman: childbearing, the care and caressing of the child, the protecting of the human form. Thus it is in all her activity: " The theme of feminine thought is not at all that which is outside of us, which often wounds and deforms us, but rather that which should be, that which is necessary in order for man

to be human and so on. . . . The moral order or the order
of perfection will be, therefore, the natural object of feminine contemplation." [33] And Alain illustrates this thought
by showing — the example is obviously a little obsolete —
that it falls to man to build the home in submissiveness to
the imperatives of physical necessity, to which he submits
all his plans; woman's place, on the other hand, is to
achieve the completion of the home's interior, following a
plan in which the ideal and imagination can be combined.
If man is the agent of necessity, woman is the agent of values. Consequently, Alain calls it, following Auguste
Comte, her power, a "spiritual" power.

This power is considerable, but does not become identical with the power of law, which is masculine. Auguste
Comte compared this power of woman to that of public
opinion, which is also a considerable power, but one that
cannot be codified. It is a power of persuasion that, it is
true, can sometimes be annulled or curbed by the juridical power, but cannot be disregarded for long: "If we define feminine thought by the function of conserving the
human form, which is naturally prone to adventuresome-
ness, if we consider this conservative function, which is
always deferred but cannot be disregarded, we will understand that this power is not and never will be enclosed
in a formula." [34] It is necessary, therefore, that man and
woman understand reciprocally the nature and authority
of the function that each of them exercises in the bosom
of the family: "Man has no need of feminine caution;
woman has no need of governing her reveries according to
the external order of which man is the agent." [35]

This myth, which Alain relates to us, would undoubtedly find confirmation in a psychological analysis that is
more profound and less dependent on a certain historical

conception that reserves work exclusively to man. This is what F. J. G. Buytendijk has attempted.[36] For him, the differentiation of man and woman has its primary source in a particular manner and capacity of being located in relation to his or her own body. Man feels his body as a means of domination, as an instrument in the service of a power of creation, of organization, and of struggle. He is *homo faber*. His ethic is one of domination over reality and of inevitable submission to this reality, which one masters only by first submitting to its laws.

Woman does not assume her body in the same manner. Her grasp on the world has something less certain about it. She shelters from the world, she preserves, she protects, more than she confronts the world. Her attitude regarding reality is symbolized by motherhood, which consists first and foremost, by means of her own body, of keeping the child out of peril. She preserves and protects. If man is *homo faber,* woman is *homo curativus.* Her ethic is an ethic of love and sacrifice. It is not by chance, let us add, that the church, as well as the nation, has been compared to a mother who protects her children and receives them when they return wounded from the struggle of life. Religious mythology abounds in figures of women who play redemptive roles. Christianity, as well, has had a great deal of difficulty in dismissing this symbolism of the redemptive woman. In Catholicism the development of Mariology or of the doctrine of the church as mediator and dispenser of grace is a sort of compensation for the renunciation of this symbolism. It is a concession to the archetypes deeply rooted in human affectivity. When one seeks to grasp the essence of woman, it is always necessary to consider her fashion of taking upon herself the world and consequently her own body, the personal mediator between the world and the self.

But, to be sure, it is inexact to conclude from this that man alone is made for work, and that woman must be confined to the care of children, of the home (including the kitchen), and to the concerns of the church. In this regard, Buytendijk makes the following remark: " As all existence is an existence in the corporeal world and as the body of woman differs more profoundly from that of man than is ordinarily thought, the type of her existence is always absolutely feminine. It is different from man's mode of living, no matter what modifications of the social structures and norms might be proposed by educational theory. This difference remains even if the woman does the same work as man. She is, certainly, *able to* work as man. In all objectivity this work is also good. The years of the war have not been alone in teaching us this. Nevertheless, experience shows (and we think that our age can better understand this fact) that woman always labors in a fashion different from that of man." [37] We will return later to this question of women working. But for the present, this notation can be of value to us. Woman can and indeed does do the work of man; she does it in a different manner. Now, especially in the modern world, it is work that is the source and manifestation of authority. To observe that both man and woman work is to credit an authority to them, but a qualitatively different authority. The problem is not, at bottom, one of knowing if man alone has authority in relation to a woman, who would owe only submission. It is one of knowing what is the quality of each one's authority.

From the myth recounted by Alain, as well as from the analyses of Buytendijk, we should bear carefully in mind the assertion, which remains true despite the evolution of civilizations, that the power of man and the power of woman are both realities, although of different nature. The power of man tends to take a more fixed, more juridical form, that is, it is sanctioned by the social order. It is a power of mediation between the social group and the family. The power of woman, on the other hand, takes more versatile, more diffuse, and more delicately expressive forms. This duality of forms is related to the duality of functions. It results from the Order of Creation, and is only partially dependent on the myth of woman created by man (a thesis defended by Simone de Beauvoir [38]). There is no doubt that this duality of authority has often been concealed in the course of history to the profit of masculine authority alone. The quality of feminine authority, moreover, puts it more and more in danger of being thus violated and forgotten.

However, in order to understand the dialectic that is established between the authority of man and that of woman, we cannot refer solely to the Order of Creation. We live in the economy of the Fall. The event of the Fall has established a tension between these two authorities: the text of Genesis concerning the domination of man and the desire that carries woman toward man means nothing other than the indication of this tension. It obviously cannot mean that man, entirely occupied with the domination of the world, is inaccessible to the desire of woman. Rather, it clearly points out that the relationship of man and woman is animated by an Eros, by a passion tainted with sin, that this Eros implies the craving in man for conquest and domination, indeed, for violence, and in woman, on the other hand, for seduction. But for both it is a question of conquest, by means of different weapons. In the world of sin there exists a secret affinity between love and seduction, love and conquest, love and war; and the poets of love, from the author of *Tristan and Isolde* to Richard Wagner, have not ceased reminding us that love has a taste of suffering and death.

It is precisely because of this situation that the juridical order of marriage must intervene, that the state cannot be disinterested in marriage, whose object is to submit the difficult relationship between man and woman to a social law. Thus one sees that it is the secularized civilizations which, because they want to ignore the sinful condition of man, accord no importance to the institution of marriage and advocate both companionate marriage and an indifferent equality between the sexes. Our reaction absolutely does not mean that Christians should, on the contrary, advocate a statute that maintains woman in her traditional servitude by depriving her of her political and social rights, by taking away from her all juridical power over her children. Rather, Christians should defend, even on the civil plane, the institution of marriage, of a marriage where the rights of man and woman are defined in reference to the diversity of the powers and functions of each one. Every civil code involves an anthropology.[39]

But one cannot stop there, for neither has the Order of Creation meaning by itself (since sin reigns there), nor can the state of sin give rise to absolute norms (since it is a transitory state already illuminated by the light of redemption). Consequently, it is necessary for us to proceed to a third reading of the Biblical texts relative to man and woman, reading them now in the perspective of redemption. It would be wrong, certainly, to suppose that redemption abolishes the Order of Creation, or that it is limited to restoring it. It fulfills it, bringing out the hidden meaning of it. Redemption tells the meaning of this common adventure that Adam and Eve have been called to live. It causes the New Creation to be perceived in the midst of the sinful creation.

The relations between man and woman are placed under the sign of this renewal and of this fulfillment of all things. There is something here that is beyond juridical relationships, even beyond ethical relationships. Paul recalls that man, because of the authority he possesses, plays a role in relation to woman that is analogous (simply analogous) to that which Christ plays in relation to every man: "But I want you to understand that the head of every man is Christ, the head of a woman is her husband, and the head of Christ is God" (I Cor. 11:3). But he hastens to add (vs. 11-12): "Nevertheless, in the Lord, woman is not independent of man nor man of woman; for as woman was made from man, so man is now born of woman. And all things are from God." Thus there is an inevitable reciprocity and a true equality between man and woman — but in the Lord, i.e., when man and woman, living in faith, are put back into their authentic existence. The New Testament knows nothing of an anthropology in which beings would be determined once for all by an immutable nature, provided with fixed and absolute attributes and functions. Man is "a being in situation," a historical being, a being who is sometimes in a false situation, sometimes in a true situation.

This is why it cannot be argued as if man were always the same, as if there were truly nothing new under the sun. This is also why there are several moral responses in the New Testament, according as one considers man as menaced with annihilation by sin and in need of preservation or man as the receiver of the hope of salvation.

It can be said, perhaps, that Paul, in the pericope of I Cor., ch. 11, when he speaks of the subordination of woman to man, is not thinking so much of the fallen man

as of the creature as he comes from the hands of God and
that, moreover, he repeats this same precept in I Tim.
2:13.[40] This is true, but even if in the Order of Creation
there is a heterogeneity of function and consequently a
difference of power, this does not at all mean a subordination of an ontological or juridical type. And even though
this heterogeneity of function continues to exist in the
penultimate economy, in regard to salvation itself there is
no consideration of differences among persons. Paul states
this very clearly: " For as many of you as were baptized
into Christ have put on Christ. There is neither Jew nor
Greek, . . . there is neither male nor female; for you all
are one in Christ Jesus " (Gal. 3:27-28). Now, where is
the true being of man, where does it become evident, unless it is in Christ? Let us remark, moreover, that this passage is part of a development in which the apostle treats
of the nullity of the law, of that law which has meaning
only in relation to sin and which must not tyrannize those
who are " dead to sin." When Paul declares that there is
no longer man or woman, this affirmation means that in
Christ (and only to the extent that they are in Christ)
man and woman are equals and equally free.

We realize that the apostle Paul is not at all concerned
with drawing conclusions from this freedom and equality
in Christ regarding the political, legal, or social order.
Quite the contrary, he sent Onesimus, the fugitive slave,
back to his master. Yet this master, Philemon, ought to receive back his slave " no longer as a slave but more than a
slave, as a beloved brother, especially to me but how much
more to you, *both in the flesh and in the Lord* " (Philemon
16). What is this to say but that, in any case (we do not
know if Paul is suggesting here that Philemon manumit
his slave), Philemon and Onesimus ought to know equality
and fraternity in all personal and social relations — and not

only when they worship the Lord together? Paul does not have the leisure to occupy himself with the question of whether this transformation of personal relations should bring, sooner or later, an abolition of the status of slavery. He has better things to do. He does not know how long the present economy will last. One cannot argue that Paul's silence on the matter means that he condemned the juridical emancipation from slavery or of women. All that can be said, concerning women, is that Paul was hostile to all egalitarianism that leveled — indeed, that forgot — the diversity of the condition of man and woman. He was hostile to all modification of the law that made of marriage a simple contract between two beings considered perfectly similar and equal in proportion to their perfect similitude. There is no place to choose between the apparently contradictory texts of I Cor., ch. 11, and Gal. 3:27-28. These texts teach neither an eternal subordination of woman in regard to man nor an effacement of the condition of woman. That the subordination ought not to be understood in a hierarchical or disciplinarian sense is shown in the parallel subordination of Christ to God (when there is between them equality of divine form, Phil. 2:6).[41]

Woman will remain, then, in submission to man, without having less dignity than he and without giving up the exercise over him and over her children of the power that is characteristic of her and without which both she and her husband forget that they are equals in the Lord. Even more, the authority of the husband, in the perspective of the New Creation, casts aside all that it has of the power of constraint, in order to become the authority of love alone, that paradoxical authority which renounces itself in sacrifice: "Husbands, love your wives, as Christ loved the church and gave himself up for her" (Eph. 5:25).

If this same pericope recalls with a veritable solemnity the tie that unites the church to its head, Christ (vs. 22-24), it must not be forgotten that this submission includes a reciprocity, since the passage relative to domestic duties is preceded (v. 21) by a general imperative that requires that brotherhood (and for Paul there is brotherhood between man and woman) be manifested in a *reciprocal submission:* " Be subject to one another out of reverence for Christ." It seems to us to be a poor method to separate this general precept, as New Testament interpreters customarily do (who are, in general, men), from the rules of family ethics.

Yet it is necessary to remark that the apostle Paul does not have the habit of utilizing comparisons in which all the terms correspond exactly. If he establishes a parallel between the relation of spouses in marriage and the relationship of Christ to the church, it is, on the one hand, in order to point out clearly that there does not exist a secular or civil order that is without relationship to the work of Christ, that there is no ethic without Christological foundations, that the essential work of Christ, the giving of himself to his own, must illuminate all our existence; it is, on the other hand, because he found in the Biblical tradition a model that served his purpose: the relationship of God to his people is always compared to a marriage. From that point it became natural for Paul, when wanting to speak of marriage, to invert the comparison and to compare the human covenant with that which God concluded with his church in Jesus Christ.

This typology does not mean that there is an exact and strict parallelism between the terms of the comparison, between man and Christ, between woman and the church. To be in the church does not mean to abandon virility! The relationship of Christ to the church illuminates that

of the husband to the wife, in the sense that it recalls to
the husband that he must love his wife even to sacrifice,
and to the wife that she must not pride herself on her
equality with man in Christ in order to assert her authority defiantly before her husband, but that she must express her love in submission. It also seems to us dangerous
to see, as does J. J. von Allmen, in the Christ-church relationship an archetype, in the full and complete sense of
the word, of the conjugal relationship, transferring quite
simply the rules that are valid for each one: the ethic of
the church is not the ethic of the family.

In effect, even though reciprocity is not valid for the
Christ-church relationship, even though the church is always and only always the body that receives both life and
orders from the head, even though the idea of hierarchy
cannot be effaced from this relationship, on the contrary,
reciprocity is perfectly possible and even obligatory in the
bosom of the conjugal union, in the Lord. It is the same
Paul who emphasizes: "The husband should give to his
wife her conjugal rights, and likewise the wife to her husband. For the wife does not rule over her own body, but
the husband does; likewise the husband does not rule over
his own body, but the wife does" (I Cor. 7:3-4). Moreover, there is this same reciprocity in the spiritual domain:
"For the unbelieving husband is consecrated through his
wife, and the unbelieving wife is consecrated through her
husband" (ch. 7:14).

We will conclude these various readings that we have
made of Scripture with the following affirmations:

1. Sanctification, which originates from the righteous-
ness of faith, transforms the relationship of husband and
wife. It does not suppress their otherness, the diversity of
their responsibilities and, consequently, their authority.
Rather, it establishes them in a perfect equality and in an

identical dignity in the Lord. In consequence, the ties of
reciprocity should, in a Christian home, prevail over the
ties of subordination and constraint.

2. On the civil and juridical level, which is also the level
of sin, the subordination of woman remains. This does not
at all come from a tyrannical will of the husband, but from
a system of law that fixes the responsibilities and powers
of man and woman. For the unity of the family it is necessary that man exercise the functions of head, which means
the functions of protector. Matriarchy (which must not
be confused with maternal lineage), of which civilizations
offer us only rare examples, would undoubtedly be an indescribable tragedy. But in this respect we are, despite all,
in the realm of the relative. Civilizations change, as does
law. At the present time, nothing prevents the juridical
preeminence of man from taking more attenuated forms
nor the reciprocity on this level from becoming stronger.
Let us not forget, when we read the letters of Paul, that
we are not dealing with a social reformer. We should bear
in mind that he was not thinking in terms of conjugal
ethics outside of and beyond the social setting of his age.

3. We are concerned about not leaving the juridical
and civil sphere to its autonomy, but, on the contrary, of
clarifying what is old by what is new, of regarding all
things in the perspective of eschatological hope. Thus it is
necessary for us to work to create a juridical order in
which the reciprocity of man and woman is asserted, to
seek for an equality that has nothing mechanical about
it, but that is attentive to the singularity of the particular
vocation of man and woman. We should not imagine that
equality is a leveling of the diversities and the richness
that the Creator has achieved in his creation.

CHAPTER V

The Social Transformations
of the Family

THE ETHICAL PROBLEMS of the family can be understood only if one pays careful attention to the social situation of the family. Such a sociological study is all the more useful since the relationships of kinship and of the family itself sometimes give us the illusion of having traversed the centuries, from the first day of the Creation up to the present, without having suffered the aftereffects of social transformations. When we speak of the family, we readily think that in the midst of social upheaval its structures remain always the same. Moralists, moreover, too often deal with an abstract, nontemporal family; they barely admit that the family is reached (they more readily say menaced) by the transformations of mores, with the result that the relationships between parents and children are no longer what they were a hundred years ago. But the transformation of intrafamily relationships is only the mirror of more profound transformations that affect the family even in its structures. We cannot isolate the family from its sociological context. Inversely, it would also be an error to suppose that the evolution of the family has always followed the same progress as that of the aggregate society which encompasses it or that the tempo of evolution is the same for family and society at large.

It is possible to perceive that the family in the Western world has not entirely followed the evolution of the society at large on at least three points.

In the first place, the modern world is composed of deeply secularized societies, that is to say, societies in which the ensemble of manifestations of the economic, political, and cultural life is no longer controlled or directly inspired by the churches. Religion has had a tendency to become a private affair. The result is that the churches, alongside other social groups, constitute differentiated societies that certainly have not lost all influence on public life, but that can no longer, in the majority of cases, exercise their influence by institutional means. They exercise their influence medially, through the go-between of public opinion or by the action of certain eminent personalities holding the reins of power in the social body.

Each sector of human activity is thus the possessor of a sort of autonomy: science no longer obeys theological imperatives; the economy obeys the laws of a system, the constraints that force it to a renewal of technological methods, the conjuncture and availability of manpower and capital; the church has ceased to be a power capable of orienting the economic life, of influencing investments, as it did between the twelfth and fourteenth centuries in Europe; political forces are secularized and obey ideologies that are themselves entirely secularized; it is only in exceptional cases that art any longer finds its inspiration and regeneration in religious motifs, for indeed it is religious art which is influenced by trends in secular art; finally, it is possible for a man to live a normal existence without ever having to submit to the authority of a church or to come to terms with it.

It cannot be pretended that the family has totally escaped this secularization. It breathes the air of the times. It is touched by secularization through the news media, culture, and the school. It is true, however, that the family is one of the rare social groups over which the church still has a direct hold. A parish is composed less of individuals than of families. The uniting of a family with a church is made most often by tacit agreement, based on a strongly established tradition more than a voluntary decision of one of the members of the family. Family ethics often bears the mark of the teaching of a church. Marriage, as a social act, is considered more as a religious act than as a juridical and civil act. Civil marriages and civil funerals are relatively rare, even in countries where secularization has corresponded to a positive dechristianization of minds. Even nonpracticing parents, or those not very faithful in their practice, or indeed totally detached from all religious conviction, consider it proper to put the education of their children in the hands of a church.

Sociology has established that the continuity of ecclesiastical life is assured by the family. In studying a parish of Lyons, France, the Rev. Father Pin discovered that "80 percent of churchgoers belong to families composed entirely of churchgoers." [42] And Canon Boulard has confirmed this observation, stating that the family "creates the extraordinary historical continuity of regions that maintain the same religious attitude over three or four centuries. It alone, in being carried on in a lineage, traverses the generations." [43] Although no similar sociological inventory has been made in Protestantism, we feel that it is possible to maintain that the number of Protestant families going back to the Reformation compose a very important part of the present Protestant population, at least in Europe.

It is precisely this function of religious social cell, placed directly under the influence of churches and assuring the continuity of the churches, that provokes permanent conflicts in the midst of our secularized societies. The political and social forces that are opposed to secularization wish to use the family as a sort of beachhead to reconquer lost positions, whereas the forces that see secularization as a cause to defend, try to destroy the cohesiveness of the family and to promote the emancipation of its members. All these facts show that the evolution of the family, even if it is strongly influenced by the evolution of the society at large, does not, however, assume all its features.

The same findings would assert themselves if one were to study a second aspect of contemporary society, its politicization. The ideological void left by the reflux of religion toward the individual and the family has been filled by politics. In employing this term "politicization," we do not mean that politics has become the ruling passion of each individual. Politicization is not incompatible with a certain political apathy. It does not exclude periods of political lassitude. A society takes on a political character when its principal standards of judgment are political, when all events (be they of the technical, economic, or even cultural order) are evaluated according to their political import, when relationships between social groups as well as between individuals are determined by political boundaries and restraints, and when the primary options before which man is placed have political consequences. Whether it is a question of production or of education, of demographic problems or of the distribution of wealth, of scientific research or of literature, we know quite well that none of these questions is politically neuter and that the very expression of these problems is related to political ideals. The family has certainly not escaped this politicization. Politics penetrates into the family circle through the newspaper, the radio, the television, animating and renewing conversation there. Political discussion is a theme of family culture. It has ceased to be a private reserve of the male. Yet however important politics might be, with the options and the separations that it entails, only in exceptional cases does it become the norm and basis of family life. The family prizes the interpersonal relationship as such. This relationship embraces all its values without any political coefficient, tolerating the different and conflicting political engagements of its members. It creates among them a sort of friendship that only rarely is jeopardized by political options. It is more easily menaced by questions of self-interest or of obscure resentments (e.g., resentments of older children against younger children) than by political ideals. In short, interfamilial relationships escape the norms of political opinion most of the time. Family cohesiveness is only accidentally imperiled by politics. When this happens (there is a pathology of interfamilial relationships), it frequently appears that the real reason is that the political reason is grafted on to more profound and rarely avowable grievances, whereas politics by itself is quite sufficient to divide cities, naturally, but also economic groups, professional organizations, cultural groups, sometimes even churches and, indeed, patriotic associations.

On a third level, the family progresses less quickly than the surrounding society, although in this respect it is not inconceivable that it can fall into line with the latter. Modern Western society has become a highly technical society and its ethics are amenable to the values of technical progress. Its dynamism is sustained by the vision of this progress. It is on the lookout for investments that favor this progress. It tends to orient instruction and education according to technical imperatives. Its structures are modified by technical discoveries. The balance of the social classes is upset by technology. A new social class has appeared, that of upper-level technicians, engineers, and top-grade employees, which even in a capitalistic system tends to become the dominant class. These are those who not only receive the greatest share of national income (they are paid even before the capitalists themselves), but still more, they are those who impose their objectives and their vision of the future on politics.[44]

Now the family, because of the limited nature of its means, and sometimes also because of the traditionalist nature of its style of living, participates in a very incomplete fashion in this technical progress. There is a considerable difference between the sight offered us by a household furnishings show and the slowness of the modernization of our homes. In this respect, there are undoubtedly many differences according to country and social circles. But on the whole one can say that the families are rare that can adopt all the appliances that modern technology puts at their disposal. There is always a time gap between the state of technology and the equipment of the home. The lag is noticed at present in questions of living conditions. In France, for example, the idea that every apartment should necessarily include a bathroom was born after the last war. What apartments these are, even in the well-to-do classes, whose conception is far from being functional, whose discomfort is obvious, and whose upkeep involves a disproportionate sum of money and human effort! Public administration and private enterprise do not hesitate to demolish buildings in order to construct modern ones. But it is more difficult to alter a family dwelling, whether it be due to one's lack of means or because it has an emotional value in our eyes. The modernization of living conditions is certainly in process, but it is an act less of the family than of the public and private authorities, building enterprises, rental agencies, etc. In a survey made in France by the review *Esprit* [45] (the survey dates, it is true, from 1953), one of the collaborators was able to write: "We lodge with our ancestors." This means simply that the living conditions of our families are rarely on the level of our present technological possibilities.

The furnishing of the interiors gives evidence of the same lag. Although radio and television have penetrated into the most diverse circles (including the working class), the appliances that would permit a substantial simplification of housework (telephone, washing machine, refrigerator, vacuum cleaner, central heating) are distributed in a fashion a great deal more sparingly. In places where distribution is more widespread (in the United States, for example), they go out of style in a manner also more accelerated. The family gets winded trying to follow the tempo of technical progress. Recourse to installment buying, whose very existence attests the technical lag of family furnishings, resolves the problem only very partially, because it produces an often catastrophic indebtedness. Such indebtedness is particularly serious in modern apartment buildings which, by their very structure, call for noncumbersome and practical, modern furnishings. Factory representatives swoop down on such buildings like vultures.

In recording that the family lags behind the level attained by modern technological civilization, we do not mean to say that the family has not progressed at all nor that it has not undergone profound transformations that mark the appearance of another style of family life. The stability of family structure is frequently only apparent.

In the first place, it should be noted that there has been a diminution in the *size* of the family. This ascertainment asserts itself not only when the present-day family is compared with its distant ancestors, the Roman *gens* or the patriarchal family of ancient Israel (types of families whose volume was that of a tribe), but when the present-day urban family is compared with the urban or rural family of the last century. Vast family dwellings have given way to small apartments with areas of two hundred and fifty square feet to two hundred and ninety square feet.[46] This reduction in surface area is not only the sign of a period of economic difficulties. It is a symbol of the reduction of the size of the family.

We mean by " family " the group composed of the married couple and minor children (it should again be emphasized that the age of majority has declined considerably). This is to say that in our very definition we cut the family off from the relations that were integrated into it in the last century. Sometimes these relations lived with the family, under the direction of a head of the family who was not necessarily the father, but who was frequently the grandfather (this was true of rural families and, among the middle class, those families that managed family industrial enterprises). Or sometimes the relations rejoined the family during periods of the year when all gathered in country residences that were veritable manor houses and small country mansions (today repurchased, in France, by Social Security and holiday camps). That these relations were truly integrated into the family is evident from the fact that their opinions weighed heavily in all essential family decisions, such as those concerning the division of legacies, the division of profits, transformations of the family enterprise, decisions of marriage or decisions concerning the choice of a profession. Today, family reunions occur only for brief periods or in exceptional cases. Nowadays this is not always the case even for events such as marriages and burials, which just a short time ago were festivals reuniting the entire family.

In actual fact, relationships of kinship have become distended. They have only an emotional value left. Quite frequently they are supplanted by relationships of neighborliness, especially in the suburban working-class milieus. For example, a recent survey, taken both among worker families living in furnished apartments and among worker families whose active members work in the same factory or in nearby factories, has established the fact that the material and spiritual care of the children and the organization of spare-time activities has been taken over by the neighborhood and no longer by the kindred. In case of family difficulties of all types (health, family breakups), as well as in cases of happy family events (births, marriages, anniversaries), it is the mutual help of the neighborhood that operates, not that of the kindred.[47] To be sure, this evolution is essentially a phenomenon of the worker class. It does not exclude, where material resources are available, recourse to a grandmother or an aunt. Yet even where the phenomenon does not take such impressive proportions, the tendency for the conjugal family to retire within its shell, to look after its own cohesiveness first, is significant. Families in which the grandfather continues as the head of the family and the patron of the family enterprise, never really permitting his sons to be-

come adults, deciding what course of studies his grand-
children will follow, seem to us a sorry and ridiculous
relic.

This withdrawal from the kinship community originated
at the same time as the rural exodus. In Europe this was
from the beginning of the second half of the nineteenth
century, when young farmers left the village of their birth
and the family community with no hope of returning.
When they settled in the cities, they broke all ties with
the family community (they could not count on vacations,
the journeys were very difficult, or they did not know how
to write, or their parents did not know how to read). It is
possible that the practice of rotating vacations and the
ease of communications will produce a tightening of ties
with the kinship community (or a rediscovery of this community). But in any case an irreversible evolution will
take place. The conjugal family will be strengthened. It
will bring about firmer ties between parents and children,
for children are generally better integrated into the small
family than they were in the larger group. The father and
the mother feel themselves solely responsible for their
children. It is quite possible that family consciousness will
emerge strengthened from this evolution.[48] The family
has gained in intimacy what it has lost in size.

The second sociological fact that dominates the evolution of the modern Western family is the emancipation of
the members of the family. The family of yesterday, rural
or urban middle class, represented a strongly graded unity,
grouped around the head of the family. The head of the
family alone assured the subsistence of the family (in the
middle-class family) or sovereignly directed the work of
the family (in the rural family). In his presence the other
members of the family were never completely adults. The

same was true of the important decisions: marriage, choices of profession, religious practice, these belonged essentially to him and were not the object of a free decision on the part of the persons concerned. This system assured a high degree of socioprofessional stability, which is still evident in rural life of today. At the present time in France a farmer's son has 64 chances in 100 of remaining a farmer. This is truly a high proportion when one considers that the rural exodus is still in process and will continue for many decades.

Stability is not as strong in the urban middle class. This is due to the progressive disappearance of family enterprises which not long ago sons entered as a sort of birthright. Nonetheless, at the present time a son from the middle class (businessmen, liberal professions, higher officials) still has 44 chances in 100 of remaining in his social class. However, this predetermination is due less to paternal authoritarianism than to the privileged condition of the son's life and education.[49]

Yet, despite this, the evident fact of the present time is the nearly complete emancipation of the wife and the accelerated emancipation of the children.

The emancipation of the wife obviously has its source in her access to professional life and consequently to cultural and social life. Various factors have led to woman's intensive participation in professional life (which, as a consequence, has affected her maintenance of the household). The ordinary reason given is the insufficiency of family resources. This fact is incontestable, especially in the worker class, and among salaried employees and small tradesmen. But if this were the sole cause, one could record a regression in the amount of feminine work in relation to the policy of high salaries that is found in some countries. But nothing of the sort is found. The American woman works as frequently as the European woman. There are, then, other more subtle causes that are brought into play. The world wars of the twentieth century have unquestionably speeded up the process, with woman coming to take the place of man in the fulfillment of economic tasks. But the end of the wars has not produced a visible reduction in the number of women who work. We must take into account the general economic picture and technical progress. Although agriculture (the primary sector) now has too many hands, due to the mechanization of agricultural techniques, and the manufacturing industry has, since 1920, tended to stabilize its manpower (secondary sector), a new field of activities (tertiary sector) has been created by the very development of industry and markets. This sector groups together all the professions having to do with the circulation and distribution of goods and with the canvassing of markets. This vast sector has unending manpower needs. It includes not only the merchants, but the army of secretaries, typists, accountants, salesmen, advertising agents, appraisers, commercial engineers, engineers of social organization, trial lawyers, attorneys, etc. Since it is still a chaotic sector (its rationalization has only just begun), it is likely that it will continue to grow.

Now, this sector offers certain openings that often require qualities of tact, discretion, courtesy in human relations, and of manual and psychological ingenuity, all of which are frequently feminine qualities. Yet, on the other hand, such openings do not demand excessive expenditures of physical energy. It is toward these careers that women are naturally drawn. Furthermore, it is for such careers that women are being prepared by an increasingly developed technical instruction that sooner or later will outclass the traditional classic instruction. Woman is thus inevitably attracted by a work in which she succeeds perfectly.

Not only is she attracted toward it, but she wants to be attracted toward it. She has access to the same scholastic formation as man.[50] She is prepared during her school years to take her place in society. Her horizons have opened to the point of cross-checking the masculine horizon. For these reasons woman has acquired a taste for professional work. And it is often necessary to disregard declarations to the contrary which women make in the course of surveys. These stereotypical declarations are the result of a traditional ethic that evolves less quickly than social structures and even less quickly than mores. Woman sighs at being forced to work, but for nothing in the world would she want to give it up.

If one were to want to divert young ladies from professional work, it would be necessary to forbid them access to the same culture as man. This is truly a dilemma: it serves no purpose to lament the large number of women who work if no measures are taken to exclude women from cultural and technical education, leaving them only with the classic studies and accomplishments. But who would be bold enough to take such a step? There is, at the present time, such an interrelationship between the culture and technology, between the culture and economic development, that whoever is involved in the culture is inevitably concerned with finding his place in the world and of participating in the common work. What sense would political rights have for women if they were outside the world of work, where political problems take on their true dimensions?

Some people would claim, to be sure, that for many

young women in the working class, who finish only primary studies, work in the factory, shop, or office is quite simply a natural necessity, and that they are incapable, at age fourteen, of justifying their choice. It is nevertheless true that work brings them a broadening of their world. They encounter there new problems, and trade unionism can offer them an opportunity for reflection.

The age of woman in the home, confined to her household duties, corresponds exactly to the age of masculine authoritarianism and, in many social circles, to a veritable slavery of woman. It is because woman necessarily participates in the upkeep of the home and its material maintenance that she has acquired a greater authority in the bosom of the family. She accedes to professional life at precisely the moment when, in our civilization, professional work has become the principal means of social and personal identification: [51] society accords consideration to individuals insofar as they are agents of production. Indeed, the human being himself sees the source of his dignity in his capacity for work. The dignity of woman has grown through her access to professional life (it has grown both in her husband's eyes and in the eyes of her children). Man is brought to share with his wife his traditional prestige as head of the family. As Andrée Vieille-Michel has pointed out,[52] the industrial revolution of our times has required a sexual revolution: the woman who works, because she has the rights and the prestige of the worker, can no longer be considered by her husband solely as a means of sexual satisfaction and as a machine for making children. She has become man's equal even in the sexual life.

Furthermore, this transformation has important moral consequences: woman, the working companion of man, realizes more easily than in the past her role as a helpmeet of man. She can share her husband's concerns and problems regarding working conditions and the trade union organization. And what is undoubtedly still more important, she shares the diversions and friendships of her husband. The formation of groups of young married couples, especially in Christian and in communist circles, even in rural areas, is a very significant social phenomenon. It means that the married couples, associated in work, remain so in leisure hours, social relationships, recreation, and cultural activities.[53] Woman takes a more important part in the decisions concerning the furnishing and modernization of the home and concerning the guidance of the children, questions that man had the tendency to decide, so long as he was the sole provider of household funds.

Inversely, the man is a bit less inclined to leave the physical work of the household and the educational concerns to his wife. Since the husband and the wife return home from work at the same time, the man can no longer demand that everything be ready so that all he has to do is to set himself down at the table. In a survey made in 300 homes in Malakoff [54] and in families in the XVI° *arrondissement* of Paris, the subject being on "the predominance of the husband or of the wife in the home," Pierre Fougeyrollas established a participation of the husband in the daily household tasks in 33 percent of the cases among the liberal professions, 37 percent in those of salaried employees, and only 19 percent on the level of merchants and craftsmen.[55]

To be sure, these facts should not be generalized. For one thing, they vary according to the social classes: among lawyers and in the liberal professions one notices rather a total resignation of man, even in questions of education.

Nevertheless, these facts mark a new tendency that is likely to continue and that the churches can accelerate.

Proportionally as the rights of woman and her authority are better recognized and where her dignity as an adult is no longer questioned, there has been a loss in the aggressiveness of the feminist claim. The age of the suffragettes, and indeed of the " tomboy," is past. Woman is less tempted to advocate an unqualified egalitarianism, with its resultant loss in femininity. When all careers are open to woman, she exercises selectivity among them. In fact, she does not seek to avail herself of all the possibilities that are open to her.

The number of women who work is already considerable in our society. In France, in 1945, the number reached 30.8 percent of the total female population between fifteen and sixty-five years of age (not including agriculture) and 34.8 percent of the total active population.[56]

It remains true, however, that woman's access to professional work, which has been the cause of her emancipation, also poses serious ethical problems in the home. The first of these problems is the extreme weariness of the modern woman who adds her housework to her professional work. This difficulty can be mitigated only by the cooperation of her husband and, above all, by more modern equipment in the household, which would save time and decrease her fatigue.

But the most serious problem is the lot of the child. In early childhood as well as in adolescence, the empty home constitutes a great danger for the child. There are, of course, objections to the physical disadvantages (children left to themselves, older children assuming enormous responsibilities in relation to younger brothers and sisters, children left with neighbors or, indeed, left purely and simply in the street, the absence of all parental control over the schoolwork of the children, the absence of collaboration between the family and the school). But the psychological and moral disadvantages should be emphasized even more. Psychoanalytic studies have shown how essential is the affective tie that unites the child in early childhood to his mother. If the child is entrusted to a neighbor or to a day nursery, a traumatism can result whose consequences will come out later in mental disorders.

Regarding the child in the course of the first year, Colette Hovasse emphasizes the necessity of maternal presence in these terms: " The mother is for the child at one and the same time the first object, in the philosophic sense of the word, that permits him to become conscious of himself as a subject, i.e., as an entity different and distinct from that which surrounds him, the mediator who transmits the external world to him, feeds him, changes his diaper, and talks to him, and above all, the stimulator that makes it possible for him to progress." [57] When the child is older he has need of finding someone in the home in whom he can confide, recounting his little problems and experiences. The home that is empty during a large part of the day is indeed one of the major arguments that can be advanced against the work of women.

However, at the present time the involvement of women in the world of work is bound up with a physically and morally irreversible evolution. The question is how we can reconcile the contradictory necessity of woman's participation in the complete social life and the necessity of her presence in the home. The only solution seems to be a limitation of the duration of her work. One immediately thinks of part-time work. But, in fact, the labor market offers very few situations of this type. Part-time work is not viewed favorably by employers because it complicates considerably the functioning of the enterprise, hindering the continuity of the work. Yet it also constitutes a reserve of manpower that can be utilized in peak hours and can be one of the factors in the organization of rotative shifts. But part-time work frequently deprives full-time workers of overtime. Women part-time workers are sometimes exempted from the most tedious labor (cleaning up), and also are more prone to accept less favorable financial arrangements, thus practicing a sort of unfair competition. Finally, the women who engage in part-time work are not without criticisms of the system. Part-time work nearly always involves inferior jobs. There are no possibilities of further professional training or, as a consequence, of advancement. What is more, it does not pay very well. In general, nowadays, it is the type of work that has a tendency to be routine. It is possible that it constitutes only a lesser evil.[58]

There is another solution that should receive the attention of specialists in the field. This is the interruption of work for the married woman with younger children (usually when she is between twenty and forty years of age), with a resumption of work coming when the home absorbs less of her time. This resumption of work would come at the time of woman's full maturity, at the time when, psychologically, she feels a need for a renewing, for a dedication to a cause that goes beyond her home (this is an age when the middle-class woman becomes active in charity organizations or embarks on the social life). This is also the period when the material needs of the home increase and continue to increase (with the extension of the period of schooling of the children). This system would have extremely favorable consequences, but, of course, its framework is dependent on certain conditions (it is purely experimental at present, but it has been carefully studied and recommended by the World Council of Churches' Department on Cooperation of Men and Women in Church, Family, and Society). First of all, it is necessary that the young mother who quits her job retain a certain number of rights for the future in the office or firm that employed her. Secondly, it is necessary that the management (which has an interest in it) arrange brief but frequent periods of further training in the course of the years during which the work is interrupted. In this way the women will not lose contact with their professions and will be interested in the perfecting of techniques, so that at the proper time they will not have to begin from scratch. In other words, it is necessary to promote a spirit of initiative in society, to pay the price for the social promotion of women. But the stake is worth it. The idea that women should return to being occupied solely with their household duties is an idea as utopian as the return to cottage industry.[59]

The accelerated emancipation of youth constitutes a fact that is undoubtedly less spectacular, but not less critical. Here again education must be considered as one of the essential causes of the phenomenon. The school takes the child from the family and introduces him to a world of horizons more vast than the family horizons, giving him a taste for participation in the collective life. But school involves all sorts of extracurricular complements which, since the end of the nineteenth century, have formed one of the newest aspects of our life. At a very early age the child has his own activities. These activities are his own affair, at least partially outside of the control of the parents (youth clubs and movements, clubhouse and, on occasion, bands of youths and gangs of adolescents). Although gangs of adolescents are of a pathological order, they have the same meaning as youth movements. In this respect we are again in the presence of an evolution, so important that governments are forced to have a youth policy, to invest considerable sums in the equipping of youth establishments.

This term " youth policy " would have been completely incomprehensible and ridiculous forty years ago. The entrance of the child and of the youth onto the historical scene is a recent event. It means that our civilization, which had only indifferently taken note of the child over the centuries, has discovered that the child also is a person, with the rights of a child. We have discovered that the integration of the child into the social life does not belong to the sole initiative of the family, which is always preoccupied with guarding the child for it. In actual fact, the emancipation of youth is quite often brought about outside of all social organizations.[60] This is a problem with which the state must be preoccupied (but with a certain discretion, in order that youth is not involved prematurely in a political outlook). On the other hand, it is indispensable that the churches increase initiatives.

In any event, youth is considered as a particularly dynamic political addition and is thus solicited by a particular political and social appeal. The most influential parties organize youth branches. It is youth (college students, but also high school students) who form the *avant-garde* of revolutionary movements, whether it be in Hungary (1956), in Algeria, or in Cuba. It is quite possible that the idea of lowering the voting age from twenty-one to eighteen, an idea advanced shortly after the Second World War, will one day be accepted; if one is capable of being a soldier, one is capable of being a voter. The lengthening of the period of schooling, envisaged or realized by numerous governments, will result in increasing the political maturity of young people. Some actual experiments have already been made, e.g., the creation in certain cities of paramunicipal commissions for youth, which offer the possibility to young people of participating in the administration of municipal affairs and of initiating youth into the functioning of the machinery of city government.

It should be added that young people acquire financial autonomy more rapidly (salaries of apprentices and trainees, scholarships, presalary) and that, in consequence, they are called upon sooner to take responsibilities that have always been considered as belonging to adults.

Finally, the freedom of relationships between young men and women, which can also be ascribed in great part to the school, makes the choice of a husband or wife something closer at hand. The parents intervene less and less, and further, it is not always the young man who necessarily has the initiative. The average age of marriage tends to become lower, an obvious sign of the accelerated emancipation of youth.

From this fact, the integration of youth into the family has ceased to correspond to a state of fact guaranteed by mores and tradition. This integration must be achieved by the family itself, and this depends on its capacity for reception as well as on its openness to the world.

The intervention of public authority in family life is the necessary consequence of the diminution of the size of the family and of the limitation of parental authority. For a very long time in the Western world the family was considered as an autonomous society in relation to the civil authority. The rights of the father were considered as natural rights and, consequently, unlimited, the father being accountable only to God. This long-standing idea, the heir of Roman law (to which Christianity puts its seal), has not been able to resist the evolution of customs. The family nowadays knows that it needs the aid and protection of the state. It is only natural that this aid and protection be accompanied by an element of control. Immersed as it is in the surrounding society, the family is too weak to do without this protection and supervision. No longer being able to count on the unfailing support of a vast community of kindred, it could not face all the demands of civilization and technical progress. Thus it turned to the state, claiming the state's assistance as a right. It is necessary to recognize, moreover, that the modern state, which has become more totalitarian, could not dissociate itself from the manner in which the family assumes the keep and education of its children. Based on a democratic organization (and democracy implies a certain totalitarianism), it wants the family to furnish it with informed citizens, capable of exercising their political responsibilities. Since it is responsible for the national economy, it wants to have efficient producers in sound health. As a consequence, its intervention can be seen essentially in two areas: education and health. Its intervention has become all the more necessary because health and education have become very expensive items.

Although the state is interested primarily in the child, it is compelled by degrees to take an interest in all the members of the family, for the child cannot be isolated from the family circle. His physical, psychological, and moral health depend immediately on this circle. Consequently, the human being is taken in charge by the state even before his birth, and the protection of the state accompanies him throughout his life. Prenatal clinics, practically obligatory for salaried employees, infant welfare centers, obligatory vaccinations, compulsory education, school medical supervision, placing of the sick or mentally defective child under special care, vocational guidance, open-air camps, psycho-pedagogical centers, prenuptial medical certificates — these are only some of the institutions that point out the manner in which the state proposes to make its intervention in the family secure. It tries to make the family cooperate, whether it likes it or not, in the work of civilization of which the nation has charge. In order to do this it does not hesitate to utilize methods of constraint regarding recalcitrant or simply negligent fathers. When necessary, it will take the child's defense against the parents, it will respect the rights of the child (e.g., over his inheritance), and will limit the right of paternal correction. It will set about assisting the incompetent mother through a social welfare worker and will put family allowances under guardianship. It will take away, in serious cases, the right of guardianship or tutelage from one or both of the parents and, finally, will decree the loss of paternal rights.

It will be observed, however, that this function of supervision, coercion, or surveillance also has a positive side. The state puts at the disposition of the family a network of social services, family allowances, educational scholarships, construction subsidies, housing allowances, and so on. The grouping of families in cooperative associations is, moreover, a suitable means for the families to benefit freely from the possibilities that are offered to them, and to do so without administrative difficulties. Finally, the state also intervenes in cases of need to relieve the family of expenses that overburden it because of illness, industrial accidents (workmen's compensation), or the presence of aged or infirm members.

All the institutions together, which currently mark the degree of civilization of a nation, have progressively engendered a completely new frame of mind. The families themselves count on this aid and protection. They call for the augmentation of the welfare budget of the state in order to permit an extending and perfecting of preventive as well as curative measures. The state tends to become, following a formula presently popular, a welfare state, a state that provides for the most diverse family needs and even prevents them. The Roman Catholic Church, so concerned for the authority of the fathers of the family and for family autonomy, does not hesitate to recognize that there is a theological basis for this subordination of the family to the public power. The encyclical *Divini illius magistri* declares: "The family is an imperfect society, because it does not have in itself all the means to attain its own perfection, whereas the civil society is a perfect society, having in itself all the necessary means to a particular end, which is the common good. Thus under this aspect, viz., in relation to the common good, the civil society has preeminence over the family. The family finds precisely in the civil society the temporal perfection that is suitable to it." This declaration does not mean that the Roman Catholic Church is ready to accord to the state, as guardian of the common good, all the rights that it claims over the education of children. Yet the statement is nonetheless representative of a widespread attitude: the family needs to be protected, supervised, and, if necessary, constrained by the civil authority.

Is this cause for alarm? Undoubtedly the totalitarianism of the state is a menace that cannot be taken lightly. The imperatives that determine its intervention are of an economic, technical, and ideological order, and these themes do not necessarily describe the common good. Moreover, the common good cannot be defined in a purely objective and scientific manner. The common good is always defined through the means of a fundamental ethical option. This can be in error and nothing guarantees us that the state will discern clearly in every case the good of the human person. The concern to improve the material quality of the nation that currently leads the state to improve its health facilities and its measures of social prophylaxis, to intensify the battle against alcoholism, can also lead tomorrow to the liquidation by euthanasia of useless mouths, the sterilization of certain individuals, and the day after tomorrow to the generalizing of methods of artificial insemination. The concern to foster demographic balance can lead the state to a policy of encouraging large families, but it can also lead to a policy that makes abortion a perfectly legal process. The idea of the welfare state represents a dangerous utopia exactly because it implies that the state discerns the common good with a perfect lucidity.

This call for Christians and the churches to be vigilant regarding the policy of the state must not, in any way, lead us to condemn the intervention of the state in family life. We cannot refuse to recognize that this intervention has had, in general, a beneficent character and has been for the good of the child. To this policy, in particular, we owe the decrease in the rate of infant mortality in France (in the course of the first year of life) from 66 percent in 1936 to 41 percent in 1952. It is also responsible for the generally effective protection of infants and adolescents against illness (notably tuberculosis), against ill-treatment and cruelty, and even against the danger of moral corruption. We owe to this policy many efforts that have been made to rehabilitate psychopathic children, mental defectives, and juvenile delinquents, and to give them a place in the life of society. The family is incapable of giving the necessary reception to the child and of preparing him to fulfill his social function.[61] The institution of social security is one of the most remarkable social gains to benefit the family. Thanks to social security, the family can take advantage of progress in medicine and surgery. This progress comes at such a high cost that the family would not be able to participate in it in the majority of cases if it could not count on the interdependence of the nation.

It is evident that each establishment of social security and providence involves a moral risk. This risk is that the individual, instead of assuming his responsibilities as father of the family, will resign his responsibilities and turn toward the collectivity. It can even happen that the individual will no longer be concerned about taking initiatives, and will wait for them to be taken for him (e.g., by the social welfare worker).

But the role of the social worker is not only to bring a given amount of necessary aid to the family. Rather, the social worker's role is, on the one hand, to make " easier the reciprocal adjustment of structures and individualism," [62] and, on the other hand, to help individuals and families to participate in the social effort. " It is necessary that the present or potential beneficiaries of social action be associated in the continuing efforts, in the administration of social welfare, and even in the exercise of social action." [63]

The institution of compulsory and free schooling has not dispossessed parents of their responsibilities regarding the intellectual development of their children. No more should the existence of social welfare necessarily kill the spirit of initiative and responsibility, at least not if the organization is aware of the need to associate the beneficiaries in its management and in its progress, including their share of initiative in its customary functioning. It is necessary that there be semiofficial bodies between the families and the state-controlled institutions. These semiprivate groups will permit an effective collaboration of families. This is the explanation of the parent-teacher associations, family associations, and the various cooperative groups that are such a characteristic social phenomenon of our time.

Precisely because the churches exercise such a direct influence on families, they should aid families to reflect on the meaning of these institutions, to develop among them a taste for what can be called the social adventure. Péguy styled the father of the family as the great adventurer of modern times. Up until the beginning of this century the father of the family has known this adventure in a purely individual and individualistic fashion. It is now necessary for him to cooperate on a collective plan. The adventure operates on a different level, but it has not ceased to be an adventure. The lofty scruples that were expressed at the time of the debates on social security at the National Synod of the Reformed Church of France in 1947 (Synod of Mazamet), scruples concerning the recourse to social security made by Christians and pastors, are certainly not devoid of all basis. Yet they are obviously still an outdated attachment to a bourgeois individualism. Every social institution of the social security type involves a possibility and a risk. The moral problem does not arise on the level of the institution itself, but in the use that is made of it. The individual can be a passive instrument in the hands of a state that is proportionally more dictatorial as the individual is less conscious of his responsibilities. But he can also be a conscious and informed partner of the state. The difference depends on the moral formation given to the modern citizen.

In this regard it should be pointed out that the ethical preaching of the churches has remained far too individualistic. It cooperates only indifferently in the formation, on the level of present social institutions, of modern man. The upstanding father of the family is always the faithful spouse who loves his children. But he is also the supporter of family associations, of cooperative groups, of parent-teacher associations, and the voter who does not ignore social elections.

CHAPTER VI

The Present-Day Functions
of the Family

I N THIS CHAPTER we will try to catalog the functions that, by priority, the family must guarantee and to which it must devote an informed attention.

The first fact that intrudes upon us, however, is that the family, in losing some of its volume, has lost a certain number of its functions. Moreover, the functions that it has lost are those which had a particularly evident social incidence, those which were easiest to catalog.

The function that the family has long since lost, mainly because of Christianity, is its religious function (insofar as it was a question of an autonomous function). In antiquity the family was a social cell, as *La Cité antique* of Fustel de Coulanges has shown so well. The family had its gods, and the father of the family was the priest of the family. Yahweh appears to us in the Old Testament as the God of Abraham, Isaac, and Jacob, that is, as the God of a family. Christianity, in proposing for our worship a God in whom all the families on earth are blessed, has definitively set aside all tribal or familial representation of God and in consequence has deprived the family of all religious autonomy. To be sure, the family continues to exercise a religious influence. It is the initiator of infant piety, although it works under the control of the church and in fidelity to the teaching of the church, and it extends its action with the means and according to the methods that the church teaches to it. Family worship can no longer be anything but an echo and a reflection of the worship of the church. Ancestor worship, which had its basic source in the family, can be followed only in a disguised, clandestine, or sentimental fashion: the worship of the dead is scarcely evident anymore except at All Saints' Day. And modern taste, combined with the smallness of apartments, has tended to bring about the disappearance of those galleries of ancestors' portraits (formerly trimmed and decorated with flowers on holidays and anniversaries) which are the last hesitant vestiges of the worship of fathers, with the portrait of the ancestor surmounting an altar. Not only has the father lost all sacerdotal function, but with the growing secularization he has unfortunately tended to abandon his functions as religious educator to his spouse.

The political function resisted longer than the religious function. In fact, even in the modern Western world, political contests have been struggles of influence between families. The dynastic idea is nothing other than the projection, on the level of the city, of a family myth. But the democratization of political life and the break in the political cohesion of the family have resulted in the conferring of political responsibility on the individual. The frequent denunciation of nepotism shows how sensitive public opinion is on this point; family ties must not influence political affairs. There are certain sectors of values that must not intermesh, and it seems absurd and ridiculous to us that political labels can mask (as sometimes in Corsica, for example) only old family rivalries. The father, as head of the family, can certainly profit from social advantages related to his responsibilities, but he cannot draw a supplementary political authority from his position. The often advocated idea of the family vote clashes with our feeling for justice and runs counter to all democratic evolution.

The juridical function persisted longer than the political function. It has not disappeared without leaving certain traces. For instance, the father is held legally responsible for debts contracted by his wife and for damages or accidents caused by his minor children. But he is no longer held responsible for misdemeanors. The right of paternal correction is recognized by law, but it can be exercised only within certain limits and is supervised more and more closely. We are far from the age where the father had the right of life and death over the members of his family. The state reserves to itself the right of taking the delinquent or perverse child from the control of the family. Legislation has deprived the father of the right of disinheriting his children. On the contrary, it controls the father's administration of property that belongs personally to the child.

On the economic plane the family has remained an autonomous consumer cell in the majority of cases, despite the limitation introduced by the existence of school lunchrooms and industrial canteens. The requirements of modern city planning can, assuredly, imperil this privilege. It is not impossible that a policy of construction will be developed in the future that will abolish family kitchens in favor of a community restaurant. Economically, the family is obviously a nonprofit enterprise and the collective kitchen would represent a gain of money and, more especially, a considerable gain in time. The peril is not chimerical. In an age where economists and city planners appear as the all-powerful masters of the city, it is necessary to denounce this peril before it has taken shape. At a period in history where professional life is particularly intrusive, where even Sunday peace and quiet is jeopardized, it is necessary to defend the family meal. The family meal is the fundamental institution of the family, the occasion of family cohesiveness, a veritable sacrament of family life.

Although the family has remained a consumer cell, it is quite evident that it is no longer a cell of production. It no longer represents a production group. To be sure, the family has remained a production group on the level of small family enterprises (family farms and small businesses), that is, on the level of the most archaic and least well equipped forms of production. But for this reason they are destined to disappear gradually, whether it be in favor of great industrial enterprises, in favor of cooperative farms, or in favor of a more rational and less costly distribution of goods.[64] This evolution will come about for increasingly large groups of people, from the disappearance of family patrimony. The family will seek more and more to transmit to its children a faculty for work rather than a family fortune. Consequently, this fortune will be utilized in the building of a professional formation rather than in the accumulation of goods to transmit. The family, certainly, will continue to play a certain role in the maintenance and transmission of personal and real estate. Also, the state supervises even the exercise of this function, insofar as these goods belong likewise to the national patrimony (thus, for example, there are stipulations concerning the upkeep of real estate and the resurfacing of building facades). But, as a matter of fact, in doing this the state constrains the family to transform its fortune into a sort of social investment and reminds it that it lives not for itself but for the city. When one considers the burden that familial egoism has exercised on economic life, it must be recognized that this evolution is not catastrophic. This is true especially when it is accompanied by an effort on the part of the state or of collectivities to give youth, whatever be their origins, more equal chances in life (freer access to various levels of instruction, attempts to promote the social status of work).

In the light of these remarks, what tasks remain peculiar to the family? This problem is important, for the vitality of the family is tied to the diversity and to the worth of the tasks that are offered to it. A family deprived of all functions would be doomed. Emotional values alone would not have the power to preserve its existence. If these emotional values are not tested in the execution of common tasks, they lose all dynamism.

It goes without saying, to be sure, that the family has first of all a biological function of reproduction. It is not easy to see how the family could be supplanted in this task. Of course, it is possible that, sooner or later, methods of artificial insemination, indeed of impregnation *in vitro*, could call into question this function and this basic meaning of the family. If this were to happen, we would have a good example of technological progress calling into question the most profound traditions and the fundamental values of humanity. But the fact of reproduction does not in itself constitute the specific character of the human family. The animal family exists only for reproduction. Its duration is strictly conditioned by the biological process of reproduction and by the biological needs of the newly born animals.

Human existence takes form in a specifically human setting, which is constantly renewed under our eyes by the progress of techniques of living conditions, comfort, and hygiene. The family is constantly in need of assistance in the formation of this home, yet it is nonetheless true that it is on the initiative of the family that the building of the home depends, that receptive type of home which protects life and health. There is no authentic family where there is not a possibility of realizing a stable physical environment. It is not by chance that families which are obliged to live in furnished apartments present a more marked degree of instability than families that we can properly call normal exactly because they have been able to build permanent material homes which belong to them. We should also point out the difficulties that young married couples encounter when they are obliged, because of the housing shortage, to live with their parents.

We can understand from this that the idea of patrimony is intimately associated with the idea of family. This association is so vital that communist countries, in destroying or in considerably limiting patrimony and the possibility of transmitting it from generation to generation, have first of all believed that the family had lost its *raison d'être*. To be sure, in an industrial civilization that necessarily tends toward certain forms of collectivization and planning, family patrimony loses its importance. It no longer constitutes a decisive factor of economic life and no longer determines the legal rules and the ethical outlook of the family. Since considerations of amassing capital have lost their importance, marriage has become a free act of the partners.

Nevertheless, even though the economic significance of patrimony has been greatly modified and even though patrimony has been reduced to ordinary pieces of furniture for more and more numerous strata of the population, the family still continues to maintain, manage, and improve this reduced patrimony (furniture and houses). It rediscovers, on this modest plan, a certain economic function.[65] It is the collective work of the family to increase the comfort and sometimes the value of objects in common use, to improve and modernize living conditions in order to prevent the family house (when the family owns it) from losing its value (either from dilapidation or from the preservation of too obvious traces of an age gone by). The work of the family is also to give a personal worth to material objects, to confer on them a human value and an emotional increase, to permit them to be preserved in the family line. Here again it is necessary to underline that the rapidity of technical progress devalorizes, sometimes inexorably, the material objects, and that the size and style of modern apartments frequently forbids the transmission of furnishings from parents to children.

Generally speaking, a civilization in which plastic and its derivatives tend to replace metal and wood and in which it is advantageous to resell the car at the end of two or three years no longer permits, as in the past, such a general attachment to objects bequeathed by the preceding generation. This brings about an increase in the dicontinuity between generations, and the family, as well as the individual, lives in a world that is less stable than in the past. The weakening of the idea of patrimony means that the family no longer finds, or will find less and less, in the preservation of patrimony the reason for its own existence. It will oppose with far less resistance the changes in the economic and social structure that can be produced.

Freed, in a very general way, from its function of conservation and from the management of a large capital, the family will devote all its energies to that which constitutes its primary task, the education of children. But here again it is quite necessary to observe that it is no longer alone in the work, that it can no longer claim an absolute privilege in this realm. The school shares the educational effort with the family. It relieves the family of an important part of education, namely, of the instruction.

Instruction cannot, moreover, be completely isolated from education, as is sometimes wrongly believed. In effect, instruction is an education of the senses, of the intellect, and of the will. It leads to a mastery of the self, to a discernment of what is true, to the habit of avoiding what Bousset called the greatest derangement of the mind, viz., to take as true what one would like to be true. And, as this instruction is given in the collectivity, it is indispensable that it be accompanied by an education and a socialization of the character, by an effort to help the child overcome his egoism and selfishness.

It is necessary, therefore, to lay down the principle that instruction is inseparable from moral education and to recognize that with the progress of learning, on the one hand, and of pedagogical techniques, on the other, the family must necessarily be relieved by the school. Even on the level of elementary learning (reading, writing, arithmetic) the family could not replace the school.

Yet we should remember that the family has a fundamental right, namely, that it can in any case choose the type of instruction and school that suits it. This is what is expressed by the Universal Declaration of Human Rights: " The family, by rights, shall choose the education of the child." The intention of this article is clear. It is to affirm the right of families against the arbitrariness of a totalitarian state that would want to educate and instruct the child only in view of its own ends and would be little concerned to form men with a free judgment. Although it has an excellent intention, it should be emphasized that this article does not formulate a truth that is absolutely evident. The school is not commissioned to act by the family: "Moral and intellectual culture," writes Paul Ricoeur, "does not issue, even by nominal delegation, from the family. This is easy to account for if one considers the educative content of the school on its different levels. Consider, first of all, language: it is the primary object of teaching because it is the *vehicle* of all social relationships. Now, language is a phenomenon whose structure and lines of evolution, as well as technical, literary, and spiritual efficacy, does not proceed from the family as such. The family itself is involved in and affected by the linguistic phenomenon. If it precedes the school in the task of teaching how to speak, it is only in order to transmit the rudiments of a power that goes beyond the family and that, from the very first, appeared from beyond the family.

"The same could be said for mores if one understands by this word the concrete moral law such as it is lived and practiced, on more or less differentiated levels, by an articulate society: mores are the fruit of religious influences, of customary experiences, of the reflection on what is better in life, and even of the creation of exceptional personalities. This ethical flux passes also through the family. The family gives it inward vibration and an affective warmth, but it does not form it in any radical manner.

"Finally, culture properly so-called, considered in what Hegel termed its threefold dimension of science, art, and religion, is the content par excellence of education. The family is one of its bearers, but not the creator of it. The city . . . represents the milieu whose dimensions in space and time correspond to those of language, mores, and culture." [66]

It is advisable, therefore, to be prudent and modest when one advances the alleged right of parents to give their children only the education of their choice. Culture, the principal content of this education, appertains not to the family but to the city. The school, acting on the commission of the city, brings the children to participate in the moral and intellectual values of this culture. In doing so, it sometimes reverses or calls into question the often too narrow and partial education given by the family. Parental right cannot consist of opposing this situation. But parental right does operate on another level. Parents have the right to require that the school truly create a work of culture and not one of sectarianism. The " neutrality " of the school consists neither in mutilating the national and human culture nor in cutting off the values that are offensive to the ruling power or to the reigning ideology.

It will be important, then, that families be associated more closely than at present with the very administration of the school (parent-teacher associations are only one path toward this goal). Families are the third indispensable partner that, with the teachers and the representatives of the public power, must see to it that the school assumes its full task of cultural education.

But the educative responsibility of the family is situated neither solely nor primarily on the level of social structures. It has more immediate responsibilities. It can hardly transmit knowledge and techniques, but it does build character through its community structure. It integrates the child into an intimate community life that is created from reciprocal good will, intuitive understanding, transparency, and moderated authority. It is difficult to say anything precise concerning the educative role of the family, for it is a question less of methods and techniques than of the atmosphere of the family in which its members live.[67] It is this atmosphere of trust and peace which succeeds in bringing a recognition and a love of authentic values, to which teaching can only make allusion. The family educates by slow saturation, just as it perverts by slow saturation. For this reason the parents should be extremely attentive to preserve this atmosphere and not to allow itself to be infected by irritability, dread, and anxiety, which are the usual causes of psychological difficulties among children. Of course, this atmosphere, in order to be conserved, presupposes a profound understanding between the parents. It must be a conjugal union that, although it certainly could not avoid conflicts and difficulties, would know the reality of forgiveness and would not permit suspicions, grudges, or resentments to exist. The education given by the family can have its narrowness and its lacunae; the school will be able to remedy them. But, animated by a couple that is united and untroubled in its love, this education has every chance of sheltering the child from serious psychological difficulties.

Moreover, it is necessary that the parents know to devote some time to their children. Instead of being content with giving orders and instructions and with supervising the children, the parents should realize the importance of conversing with them, of listening to them and discussing with them, of giving their experiences the depth of attention due them. The family must certainly not shelter the child from the world, but rather must think over with the child the experiences he has (the sights that he witnesses in the street, in school, at the cinema), in order to moderate the brutality of the contact between the child and the world. It must see to it that the sensibility of the child does not suffer premature shocks, which would risk seriously disturbing him, indeed, which would be traumatic for him. Of course, these shocks can come from the family itself. It is not good for the parents to allow the very young children to see the concerns and perhaps the anxieties that they themselves have. The fundamental and irreplaceable educational task of the family is to preserve the sensibility of the child and to accustom him progressively to record events. It is on the level of this protected sensibility that the family can help the child to discover and to make known his first religious impressions.

The family can also be associated with the educational activity of the school. The problem is undoubtedly a delicate one, technically speaking. Its resolution presupposes frequent personal relationships between parents and teachers. This seems to be difficult, as much from the parents' side as from the teachers', who are burdened with overloaded classes. Besides, it is not at all certain that the parents always intervene with accuracy and adroitness when they would help their children perform their school exercises. But, despite all, the technical problem is second. The thing that is most often lacking for the harmonious development of the child is quite simply the interest of his parents in what he does at school, in the discoveries that sometimes come to jolt his mental universe.

But is the family limited to educating the children? Is there not a reciprocal action, an educating of the parents by the children? We are not thinking only of that school of patience which the children make their parents attend. Indeed, if the parents consent to follow the intellectual, moral, and ethical evolution of their children, it will be given to them to live the history of a generation other than their own. The history of their children will bring about the beginning of another life, perhaps less narrow and less partial than that which they had first lived. It is certainly a test of our own pride to allow ourselves to be instructed by a generation other than our own, by a generation that we know, moreover, depends on us. Such an experience is never without profit.

Moreover, it is necessary to think of this function that the family fulfills both as a human collectivity and as a material household in relation to each of its members: it is a function that we will readily call a function of *recreation*. Professional work takes up an increasingly greater part of our lives. The tiring character of the work provokes in ever greater degree a fatigue that is more mental than physical. And piecework and simply supervisory work result in tedium. These facts lead to a debasement of human existence and call for a renewal of one's strength. If the family is able to offer its members comfortable and agreeable surrroundings, it can be the favorable place for this recreation.

However, the physical surroundings, although important, are not sufficient. The family can fulfill a recreative role only if internal tensions have been resolved, if each individual is not forced to enclose himself in an ill-tempered and jealous solitude. We bear our tensions within ourselves, to be sure. But they can be eased in our relationships with our relatives, for our tensions are nearly always the reflection of our difficulties of our relationships with our nearest relatives. Love reveals here its impotence. There is an anxious, jealous, possessive love that feeds our tensions, and there is no magic formula to resolve them. Faith, to the extent that it unveils for us the other one in his authenticity, in his spiritual future, in that which lies beyond his own character, can undoubtedly overcome the enormous difficulties of our encounter with our nearest relations, with those whom we love. But the family household can play its recreative role only if these tensions are not denied but accepted in an acceptance of others.

This recreational function is difficult to define and specify precisely. It can be expressed in the ingenious and inventive pursuit of family spare-time activities and in a utilization of vacations which are not simply a recourse to the ways and techniques that civilization offers to us. But the recreational function is not exhausted in a policy of family recreational activities.

In general, the functions that remain to the family are precisely those which a social organization can neither assume nor codify. For this reason they are difficult to specify. The modern family is called upon to invent its own functions, and to renew them for each age of civilization according to each collective style of existence.

Part Two

LOVE AND THE LIFE
OF THE BODY

IT WILL PERHAPS SEEM STRANGE TO STUDY SEXUAL LOVE
after having studied the family community. The opposite
procedure could certainly be justified. The family has no
existence outside of marriage, and marriage has no meaning outside of the love that binds man and woman. Would
it not, therefore, be necessary to present love as the foundation of the family? In departing from the logical order
we have wished to emphasize that that which makes love
human, love in its humanity, is its flowering in a specific society, the family. Human love, which binds man and
woman, can be thought of and lived in its authenticity,
outside of all romantic illusion and lack of discipline, only
in this community. Therefore the existence of this community conditions love, if not in its origin, at least in its
expression and in its finality. This is why we think that our
approach is not at all arbitrary, although it would seem to
be so at first. Human hunger is indescribable outside of its
expression and satisfaction in that social and community
rite, in that act imbued with dignity and beauty which is
the meal. So in the same manner one cannot understand
what distinguishes human love from animal sexuality if
one does not refer it to the human society of the family.

But granted that it is a question not only of instinctive

sexuality but also of human love that blossoms in community life into feelings of tenderness, affection, and
friendship that grow into fidelity, why tie the study of this
love to the life of the body? Why attach it, as we will do,
to the carnal relationship of man and woman? Would it not
be more proper to consider this love in its properly human
spirituality?

Well, we should not forget that this spiritual and moral
closeness of man and woman in the conjugal union has
something unique about it because it is rooted in a carnal
relationship that is also unique. The Roman Catholic doctrine of marriage underlines the worth of this carnal relationship in considering it as a sacrament. In effect, it is
not the priest who performs the sacramental act in marriage; it is the husband and the wife who effect it in their
carnal relationship. The use in this context of the term
sacrament can validly raise certain doubts. Yet it is necessary to recognize that the Roman Catholic Church is right
when it considers love in its carnal form not as an animal
act but as the most intimately personal act that exists. It
would be perfectly false to want to superimpose on sexual
love a spiritual love that has nothing in common with it.
This would be to involve the moral life in a perpetual
dichotomy that would make it impossible.

CHAPTER VII

The Body and the Person

TRADITIONAL Christian ethical teaching is astonishingly discreet in what concerns the body and its instincts. The various systems were based on certain anthropologies in which man is conceived of essentially as will and in which the whole problem consists of assuring the predominance of a will purified and shaped by grace over the instincts and the desires. Instincts and desires have existence only to be directly curtailed and dominated. The question does not arise of knowing if, on the level of the body, instincts, and vitality, there is not already a meaning and a mystery that should be studied with respect. Instead of wishing from the very first to correct and dominate the body by a will of iron that is insensible to the impulses of instinct, would it not be wise, abandoning all presumptuous puritanism, to try to think in terms of an ethic on the level of the body? Is there not a disturbing odor of Hellenistic gnosticism in this tendency to consider only the body as the enemy, as the rebel to subdue, as the source of sin? To be sure, the body itself does not have meaning by itself. But does it not have a meaning in the unity of the person?

There are two dangers to be guarded against in elaborating a Christian ethic. The first is the danger of confusing Stoicism with Christianity. The second is that of entering upon the way of Kantianism, as did the majority of Christian ethical systems of the nineteenth and even the beginning of the twentieth century. This latter fault consists of denying all moral significance, or even of ascribing a negative significance, to sensibility, i.e., to the body. There is a certain voluntarism that thinks itself Christian because it succeeds only at the price of renunciation. It is necessary to guard against this, for quite often it is a question only of contempt for one aspect of man, only of a refusal to give a meaning to certain instinctive and sensible functions of man, in short, of a sort of devalorization and profanation of the human creature in his unity. It is this error of perspective that explains why ethical systems that have nothing to say concerning the problem of the body, on the contrary, dwell complacently on all the questions where man appears as intelligence and will: culture, social life, and politics.

This indifference of many traditional ethical systems derives from a false conception of the relationships between the body and the person. We can ignore the flatly dualistic position that establishes a radical opposition between the body and the soul, an opposition that is made to correspond with that of evil and good. Psychology, as well as psychoanalysis and psychosomatic medicine, has produced decisive criticisms of this conception which is found in both Christian and non-Christian thought. There is a more subtle approach that sometimes conceives of the body as an instrument in the service of the person. This is exactly the fundamental thought of ancient Greece as it appears in Platonism and the cult of physical education. This thought makes an ethic of the body possible, which in the popular wisdom of antiquity was formulated in the

adage: *mens sana in corpore sano*, that is, the body, by its
health, its harmoniousness, and its suppleness, must offer
itself docilely to the spontaneity and creative liberty of the
spirit. The body is an instrument that Plato often compared to a musical instrument; it is necessary that this instrument be kept in shape. It is, among all the objects that
surround it, a privileged instrument, for it is the one that
the individual uses most and by which one gives an instrumental value to the other objects. Thus it appears that
the worth and significance of the body is considerable.
But, in reality, we have not made much progress. Considered as an instrument, the body is always outside the
person. The characteristic of an instrument, indeed, is that
it does not have by itself its own meaning. An instrument
can become the bearer of meanings that usage gives to it.
It can be forced to yield a certain return. In itself, however, it is a neuter reality and belongs to the domain of
objects. Such seems to be the last word of our wisdom
when we seek, in sports or professional training, to put
at the disposition of man instruments of great suppleness
and high productivity.

It can be immediately seen that this conception is
clearly insufficient when it is noticed that on the level of
this instrumental conception of the body one proceeds to
an *abstraction:* body in general is spoken of, not one's own
body. In speaking of body in general, it is treated as an
external reality, foreign to the person. It is reducible, as
science teaches, to certain elements that have no relation
to a personal life.

Anatomy and physiology are in one accord in doing
exactly that. And medicine, when it bases itself solely on
these two disciplines, does the same thing. The illness
then becomes more interesting than the patient. But, in

fact, therapeutic practice forces it to modify its point of view. It becomes aware that the same treatments applied in cases that are supposedly the same do not produce the same effects, as if the body possessed personal forms of reactions, as if the body refused to permit itself to be reduced to a general substance, to some nitrogenous compound, and declared itself a personal, singular, and unique reality.

Besides, death comes to remind us that the body has a partnership with our person. We can proclaim a strict doctrine of the separation of body and soul, and believe that the soul, by its spiritual nature, escapes at death. But this does not abolish the personal experience of death. It does not produce any easing of the dread of all one's being in the face of death. This means simply that we do not succeed in keeping the body in pure externality, in the anonymous and neuter realm of corporeality. We do not succeed in expelling the body outside the limits of the person. Death shows prominently, as does suffering,[68] not only that one's body belongs to oneself but that it is, at least in one aspect, oneself.

Moreover, this conviction is reinforced at each instant by the experience of one's relationship with others. It is through the body that one is for others. At the same time the individual is subjected to others, an existence that is given to others. The individual is offered to the glance of the other who seizes him, to the word of the other who reaches him. One reveals oneself to the other through the body, while at the same time hiding before him. Is not the mark and the act of presence to reveal oneself and to hide oneself? That which does not have presence — that which is simply there (the characteristic of the object is that it is there) — is exactly that which can neither reveal itself nor hide itself nor allow itself to be surprised nor betray itself. Far from the body being "the tomb of the soul," as Plato thought, it is exactly the mediator through which others become present to the individual, through which one renders himself present to others, through which one's solitude ceases. Through it and in it one's privacy is protected. Through it one's distance in relation to others is lengthened or diminished, without being able to be reduced to nothing. If the experience that we have of the death of another is so cruel and so mysterious, it is exactly because by an event that we can neither observe nor understand, his body has become a corpse. He has ceased to be a significant reality, a mediator, and has become nothing more than a thing.

It is not without interest to reflect on the fact that God himself has revealed to us the plenitude of his presence for us only in the incarnation, in revealing himself to us in the person of his Son. God did not disguise himself in a body. He has not encountered us through the means of an instrument that was the body. No, he made himself flesh to such a point that he himself is subjected in his divine person to suffering and death. Does not the body merit being called, in the words of Gabriel Marcel, "the absolute mediator"? [69] The bodily presence of the resurrected Christ in the midst of the disciples was the indispensable condition for the birth of faith in the Resurrected One, in the living Lord.

Let us say, in a general way, that all that which another wishes to be for us, all that he wishes to give or to demand of us, he gives or demands through his body, his word, his gesture, his expression. It is in our bodies that we are for the other. This contains a profound symbolism. The use of the word symbolism instead of figure, image, or allegory is a conscious choice: the body is not a collection of ciphers, a confused message that we must decipher in order to reach the person somewhere beyond the body. The body is symbolic of the person, in the sense that it is the body itself which is realized, that becomes truly and authentically the presence of the person.

The body is not a mysterious transmitting-receiving station that makes use of invisible souls to address messages to other stations which would then be interpreted according to a previously established conventional code. One does not read conventional signs in the attitudes of others. Yet one knows the other unmistakably in an attitude. Without having recourse to a system of ciphers, one recognizes another as a suffering, anguished, joyful, or deceptive being. It is possible, to be sure, to be mistaken, but this is not because one is poorly served by a conventional and inefficient system. It is because, in effect, every person is fundamentally equivocal, ambiguous, and contradictory. Each personal presence is at the same time a form of absence.

Gabriel Marcel, in analyzing sensation, has perfectly shown that it would be necessary to abandon almost every objectivist and instrumentalist conception of the body in which the body is " interposed " between the object and one's thought: " I exile myself as a disincarnate spectator of the universal mechanism which operates in the anonymous functioning of transmitters, messages, and receivers. And at the same time, there is no longer 'my body,' but a thing stripped of all personal marks. The instrument is always external to me, and even more, it is never body or organ. It is that which extends my body, that which the hand employs. Will the hand in its turn be the instrument that some corporeal soul employs? Thus at the same time that I become disembodied, my body detached from me loses its meaning and my own." [70]

The body is so much tied to personal intimacy that it permits one both to commit it and to hide it. In the act of yielding it, something of it is retained, either through bad faith or, more likely, through modesty. And it is the body that witnesses to the modesty. In the act of hiding it, one also yields it, and it is the body that betrays it through poorly hidden emotion or its awkwardness. These failures are not ascribable to the poor functioning of the body instrument, because the failures, even when they occur, are related to an intention of the person, an intention that psychoanalysis is not always capable of uncovering.

It is this tie, for better or for worse, between personal existence and the body that enables the body to find itself engaged in all the ventures of the moral life, that enables all personal ethics to be also an ethic of the body. The latter can certainly not be dissociated from personal ethics. If it is necessary to stress it, it is because the body is that aspect of one's being, that expression of one's essential personality which is most preeminently exposed, which receives all the temptations and seductions that come from others. And a temptation that rises in the heart never affects the individual without affecting him in his own body.

There is a Christian ethic of the body because the body is not excluded from the promise made to man. The expectation of the resurrection of the body signifies that the bodily life is linked to the fate of the person. It means that the body is not, as the profligate in his paradoxical concern for angelic purity would like it, a casing or an instrument whose reality can be extracted or a form of absence.

It should be noted, moreover, that even though my body

is an integral part of my person, I am not, as materialism would have me believe, my body. It is certainly in it and through it that I express my intimacy. But as I can withdraw in regard to my psychism, to my character, so can I otherwise isolate it from me, at least to establish a distance between it and me, so also can I increase or diminish the significant value of my body. I can bend it in adoration and straighten it out again in revolt, not, to be sure, as an instrument that is neuter and indifferent to what it expresses, but as an aspect of myself over which I have a hold. I assume my body. This is why I am not my body. But I can assume it more or less deeply. I can integrate it into my person, into the person that I have chosen to be; or, on the contrary, I can permit this integration to sink into vice, without it ceasing, for all that, to express my person. But in these moments of laxity it expresses the person that I am and have not chosen to be, the person that I loathe being and nevertheless am. My body is located at the pivot of the voluntary and the involuntary. It is always the revealer of my person, and never by materialistic determinism, though physical determinism, as I meet with it in pain, has a hold on it. Thus my body is evidence that the voluntary and involuntary are never separated. Without ceasing to be my body, my body is always something to be conquered. In the complexity of the situations in which I find myself involved, I can forget the fundamental intention of my existence. When this happens I say that I no longer recognize myself in what I have done, in what my body has expressed. But this is an alibi. For my body has revealed that besides my fundamental intention I also entertain other intentions, that my person is a complex of personages that are unified only by fundamental choices, the choices

of existing. The body gives the appearance of betraying
me to the extent that these choices are not maintained
(perhaps they were a form of presumption and vanity in
any case). It reminds me simply that I am inhabited by
certain personages that I would not care to acknowledge
either before God or before man or before myself. It says
that I am more than I think I am. But it in no way compels me to join with the real personage that it presents to
me objectively. Its alleged betrayals warn me only that I
am not all of a piece, that there are in me several different
characters it is impossible to ignore or deny. It cautions
me to take account of these different natures, but that I
can keep a distance in relation to them. It informs me that
I can and must establish with them a dialogue and a confrontation, a sort of permanent evolution, out of which a
decision will come if the evolution is conducted with
resoluteness and to the end. This decision is, namely, an
authentic manner of assuming myself, a style of existence,
a form of presence in the world.

My body is always linked with my person. It is not my
person. It witnesses to the distances that exist between I
and self. I can consent to my body or I can resist it, without ever denying that it is mine. I can make it participate
in projects that it would not have proposed to me, but
that it is capable of supporting. I recognize myself in it,
which does not mean that I agree with the image that it
gives me of myself, no more than I necessarily agree to my
psychological heredity, to my character, or to my psychological spontaneity.

Between the self and the I, between the body and the I,
between the psychism and the I, there is an area for the
quest of personal authenticity. My being reaches authenticity not at all by a sort of liberation of the self from an

unconscious psychological complex, not at all by a laying bare of all the possibilities (and the impossibilities) that I carry within myself, but by the discovery of a pacified unity, of a reconciliation with myself, which I can certainly not give myself, but which I can receive.

...

CHAPTER VIII

The Mystery of the Sexual Life

THESE REMARKS on the many-sided — and equivocal —
relationship of the body to the person were necessary
in order properly to situate the problem of the sexual life.
The sexual life makes evident the impossibility of limiting
oneself to the instrumentalist conception of the body. It is
impossible for sexuality to be without finality. The sexual
function is a physiological one, presenting analogies with
other functions (e.g., digestion) that psychoanalysis has
revealed. It is relative to the body, to that aspect of the
physical body which science has only begun to explore:
glandular secretions and hormonal balance. But at the
same time, it cannot be detached from the highest, most
personal manifestations of the ego. The term " love " bears
witness to this decisive and irreducible ambiguity. It un-
alterably designates a comportment that involves both
animality and a kind of spirituality.

It is true that some have wished to detach the sexual
function from all significance that can be openly acknowledged by authentic man, to take away from the sex act its
dignity. But what has been the cost of this reduction?
First of all, it has led to a ruinous dualism in terms of the
human person, an impossible dualism of soul and body
that holds up the soul and the body as two opposed and

uncommunicating substances, as if the soul and the body were not involved in each human situation.

Next, sexuality has been deprived of all significance in relation to the person. It has been permitted a meaning only in relation to the *species*, as if human sexuality had no other role than to assure the perpetuity of the species. Through his sex the human being would be simply the preserver of the species. In attaching pleasure to the consummation of the sex act, nature would have found a solid guarantee for the perpetuation of the species. If this view were correct, expressing the entire finality of sexuality, it would be at variance with our mores, our social institutions, the most fundamental advances of civilization. Monogamy would be called into question, for if it is only a matter of the preservation of the species, one can conceive of institutions less burdensome than the monogamic conjugal family. We would have to recognize either that this type of family is only an accident of history or that it is not linked with sexuality.

But there is more: this view affirms the preeminence of the species over the person. Man is at the service of the species, which is an affirmation that is at the root of all racism. This is an affirmation that is in fundamental contradiction to the Christian doctrine of the creation of man. The account in Genesis clearly emphasizes that although animal is created as species, man is created as personal being. His relationship with his helpmate is, from the very first, a personal relationship in which dialogue plays the leading role. To be sure, man has a sexual nature like the animal (at least the higher animal). But whereas sexuality remains purely instinctive in the animal, submitted to a seasonal rhythm that imperatively commands the manifestations of it, " it is freely," as Jean Jacques Rousseau put it, "that man rises to the level of animal instinct." [71] This is an excellent way to put it, for it reminds us that man does not start from animal instinct, which he strives with all the artifices of culture and language to sublimate more or less deeply. Rather, on the contrary, it is in starting from a properly human relationship, of a personal nature, that man and woman encounter the sexual relationship, not as a point of departure but as a result. The adolescent is normally first attracted by the femininity of a young girl long before he has the desire for sexual possession. The love of man and woman is born only exceptionally of a sexual encounter. Love precedes the sexual encounter, and it frequently happens that if instinct alone has carried the man toward the woman, love will not be born. Prostitution has never given birth to love; rather, it is love that leads toward the sexual encounter. Erotic literature, however little psychological truth it contains, witnesses to this very thing. Although the animal is guided by a powerful instinct that permits only a minute margin for the consideration of the individuality of the partners, man follows a completely different path. It is, indeed, a question of rising to the level of animal instinct, namely, of rediscovering it by starting from something different from it, of causing it to emerge from a more complete, more concrete, and more personal experience than that which it would give to us spontaneously.

Immorality and inhumanity begin at the moment where the sexual relation is conceived of as primary and when its fulfillment is an end in itself. For the profligate, the sex act ends on itself; not being rooted in a human encounter created from trust, affection, generosity, and the giving of oneself, it can only be indefinitely repeated with the most diverse partners until one is surfeited and disgusted with it. It is out of this disgust with the sex act that all sorts of spiritual aberrations have arisen in the course of history. It explains the obsession with a love of angelic purity, i.e., with a love that is not consummated. It also explains the obsession for spiritual espousals that were such a temptation in many Oriental religions, but that also infected nascent Christianity and is rediscovered in many sects and para-Christian utopias.[72] One is thrown necessarily into these aberrations as soon as one starts from man as animal and, with this animality as a base, tries to build a human coronation.

However, man has not been created animal, but a person destined to live in communion with his counterpart, capable of generosity and a giving of himself. He is not at all oriented toward a primordial satisfaction of his needs. Hunger offers another example of this. It is a need even more powerful than the need for sexual satisfaction. Yet in humanity it is satisfied at the end of a process that includes the concern for proportion, dignity, beauty, culinary refinement. There is a concern for sharing bread with others in a meal that is a communion in friendship and regard for the other. The maternal instinct is the same way: the mother, in one sense, only reproduces the actions and attitudes of the animal in regard to the child. It is true that the child has all the external marks of the animal. In certain respects he is essentially a digestive tube. Yet he is also a child, that is, a being with whom the mother maintains personal relationships, whom she does not suckle without smiling on him. He is a being who has, in her eyes, a destiny; he is born from her womb, to be sure, but he must be born anew at each instant in human life. He is a being who has received, or who should receive, baptism.

In the same way, we should see that the relationship be-

tween man and woman is at first a relationship of two beings who are each other's fellow creatures. Man and
woman must begin from their reciprocal friendship in
order to rise together toward that mysterious sphere in
which the animal existence is lived in a human manner.

Scholars reduce man to animal by abstraction, in order
to keep their work from becoming too complicated. Yet
contrary to their statements, instinct, with its powerful
dynamism, is not primary; if it were, all that would be
erected on it would be, in the final analysis, only an artificial superstructure that each individual or social crisis
could sweep away. A civilization that is based solely on
the repression of instincts inevitably changes into an
aphrodisiac civilization. Sublimation builds itself on repression, but allows what has been repressed to show
through, and under its sublimated forms the savagery of
instinct reappears in aberrant and pathological forms.
Even though Freud was right in unmasking all the hypocrisy of repressions and in reminding us that there is an animal in every man, he was in error in not having sufficiently
emphasized that there is a human libido, a libido rediscovered at the end of a humanization.

It should be pointed out that it is an analysis of man
that cuts man off from his humanity. It is always possible
to slip into such an analysis, because man can be treated
as nature and not as being, because nature is, in man, always the reverse of his being, i.e., his relapses, and because it is easier to observe the relapses than to grasp the
act by which man accedes to being. It is easier to describe
a human nature that comes undone, as it were, than to
describe a human nature in the process of building itself up.

This explains the origin of the constant ambiguity that

hangs over the description of sexual love. The very term
"eroticism" is charged with this ambiguity: "It can
designate first of all," writes Paul Ricoeur, "one of the
components of human sexuality, its instinctual and sensual
component; it can also designate the art of loving built
on culture and sexual pleasure. As such, it is still an aspect
of tender affection, as long as the concern for reciprocity,
mutual gratification, and giving prevails over egoism and
the narcissism of possession. But eroticism becomes errant
desire for pleasure when it is dissociated from the body of
tendencies linked by the concern for an interpersonal,
durable, intense, and intimate bond. It is then that eroticism becomes a problem. Now, we have learned from
Freud, principally from *Three Essays on the Theory of
Sexuality*, that sexuality is not simple, that the integration
of its manifold components is an indefinite task. This dis-
integration, when no longer considered as a failure but as
a technique of the body, makes eroticism the counterpole
of tender affection; in tender affection the relation to the
partner triumphs, but yet it can include eroticism in the
meaning of the sensual component of sexuality; in eroticism, however, the egoistic cultivation of pleasure oblit-
erates the possibility for an exchange of giving." [73]

This dissociation of sexuality and tender affection, this
isolation of sexuality regarding all intention of encountering the fellow being of the other sex as a person, obviously
remains a permanent possibility. It is the counterpart of
the intellectual vice of abstraction. It is the analogue of an
intellect that is not disinterested, but that is dilettante,
refusing all commitment because it has beforehand sup-
pressed all conditions for a commitment. There is a pro-
fligacy of the spirit, an intellectual eroticism, just as there
is a sexual eroticism.

It is because man experiences this possibility, which constitutes a major temptation, that he is so inclined to tie sexuality to evil and to weight it down with so many complexes forbidding him to speak of sexual love. Having recognized the evil in sexuality, occasionally interpreting the account of the Fall as the account of the first sex act, he develops a kind of Satanism of love, much in the manner of Baudelaire, who at least had the courage to admit: " As for me, I say: the unique and supreme delight of love lies in the certitude of doing evil. And man and woman know from birth that all sensual delight is found in evil." This is truly a strange aberration: the encounter of man and woman in sexual love no longer concerns they themselves. It no longer has any aim except their communion in evil.

Although man, once he has liberated Eros from all ties with the person, rarely engages himself in this satanic course, he nevertheless suffers a repeatedly disappointing experience of the poverty of Eros. Sexual pleasure, when it is not tied to tender affection for a person loved in body and soul, does not possess the secret of its renewal. The imagination is drained in trying to renew it: " Here is man," writes Paul Ricoeur, " engaged in an exhausting struggle against the psychological poverty of pleasure itself, which is scarcely susceptible of attaining fulfillment in its biological savagery. Eroticism will then construct its myth in the period of self-indulgent dissociation and within the limits of affective finitude." [14] Civilization, in its aphrodisiac aspects, seeks to renew the sources of pleasure, to vary the conditions of it, and to heighten the intensity of it through refined preparations. Its incessantly renewed effort witnesses to its failure. Man is thrown back toward solitude by pleasure itself.

It is understandable under these conditions how humanity, taught by the failure of the sexual myth, has come to disparage love, to consider sexual instinct degrading, and why it has been loaded down with all sorts of restraints and prohibitions. We can understand why, in these conditions, the best service that poets and novelists can render to a humanity fatigued by its own eroticism, is to sing, if in extremely crude terms in the manner of a Giono, the marvel of love and tender affection, of the gratuitousness of this gift, of the liberty of a love released from all prohibitions that a civilization both prudish and aphrodisiac (prudish because aphrodisiac) has laid upon it.

We said " in the manner of a Giono," but also in the manner of The Song of Solomon. The Song of Solomon, far from having the theological and allegorical meaning that is ordinarily given to it in order to justify its presence in the Biblical canon, sings quite simply of human love, of demythologized conjugal love, i.e., of love freed from its religious concerns, from its sacred meaning (which it borrows in order better to hide itself and sublimate itself in the pagan hierogamies). In commenting on The Song of Solomon, Daniel Lys writes: " Eros has an end in itself. It is not utilitarian, and this is why it is fidelity (exactly as the love of God is fidelity). . . . If love does not have an end in itself, the other is only an object subordinated to the end pursued. This object is worth nothing in itself. It is valuable only insofar as it helps attain the end desired. It is abandoned when another, better, presents itself." [75]

At the beginning of this chapter we protested against an interpretation of sexuality that seeks its utilitarian justification in its social function (procreation, the preservation of the race or of the species, the temporal extension of man in a lineage). This protest was made not because we

contest that marvelous aspect of sexuality which enables
us to go beyond ourselves through procreation. Rather, it
is because in putting this function first, man risks seeing
in woman nothing but the mother of his children. He risks
degrading her into an instrument that permits the survival
of his line. There is a bourgeois ethic of love that is no
less perverse than the ethic of the profligate, viz., that
ethic which, sometimes inspired by a certain puritanism,
wishes to see in woman only the *genetrix*. But it is obvious
that, in this view, all women are the same, provided that
they give an heir and, above all, a male heir. It is equally
obvious that love would then lose all personal character
and that, by this very ethical bias, one reintroduces into
sexuality that profound dissociation from tender affection,
friendship, and respect.

"Human sexuality," writes Th. Bovet, "is integrated
. . . into an order of things in which it has its place. It has
its own meaning as a creative function which is fulfilled
in the order of love." [76] Of what creation is it first of all a
question? It is a question of the creation of the other and
of the self in the mystery of a communion in which solitude is not, to be sure, conquered once and for all, but in
which it appears as provisional and not absolute.

The assertion that sexual relations must not take place
outside of marriage is frequently presented to us as a sort
of social necessity, as a discipline that is initially imposed
on us by the group as a safeguard of order and that even-
tually we impose upon ourselves as proof of the strength
of our will over the impulses of our instincts. These are
sound arguments, but they are also insufficient. The ethical foundation of the prohibition of adultery is far more
profound.

Each human being is involved in a multitude of relationships in which his personality is built (or possibly destroyed). He is a being of relationships. But man preserves his personal singularity in these relationships (which expose him and make demands on him) only in forming or in discovering within himself, through these very relationships, an inward being that cannot be surrendered to all and sundry, that must be held back. And the more intense our relationships with others become, the more we feel the necessity and the value of reserve and modesty. This is why we make a selection among our relationships that marks the limits of our availability to others. We choose our friends, certain intimates to whom we surrender a part of this hidden mystery of ourselves. But none of our friends can know us perfectly.

However, this hidden being, which is our own mystery yet which we suspect that we ourselves know only imperfectly and whose revelation we await in some way, cannot be maintained unexpressed. Otherwise it wilts and dies. We cannot make our own private use of it by some type of refined egoism. Narcissism is the trap of the discovery of the self. This hidden being, which must be revealed to ourselves and which must be made fertile, must also be offered to someone. In friendship we find something of this giving of the self, but in friendship it is not without reserve and reticence. The occasion of this unique giving of the self, of this revelation of the self in the bosom of the conjugal couple, is love. The relationship of man and woman in the midst of the conjugal couple is nothing other than the realization of this unique mutual giving of the self. It is an exclusive relationship where the mystery of the one is offered to the mystery of the other, where man discovers himself in discovering his wife.

This unique and irrevocable experience does not have,

it is true, a purely sexual character, but the sexual aspect is a necessary part of it. An unconsummated marriage is not a true marriage. It does not create between the " conjoints " this unique and exclusive intimacy. For sexuality has a way of expressing all the mystery of our incompleteness, all that expectation of the other that witnesses to the fact that man is fully himself only in the unity of the couple (he was created male and female!). Because sexuality is thus tied to the giving of the self, and to the extent that it is so, it participates in this intimacy of being. It is aberrant only to the extent that it is not integrated into this intimacy and that it, consequently, cannot participate in this giving, in this unique and unreserved generosity that binds man to woman.

Sexual relations between man and woman have human significance only as the sign and the fulfillment of a personal relationship so profound that it must be unique. It is precisely this necessity which explains the bond between love and fidelity. It explains why love in its intention wishes itself faithful. And this fidelity, which is first of all fidelity to the other, is also fidelity to oneself. Man respects his own intimacy only in his fidelity to his wife. Infidelity signifies not only that the individual does not respect the person who has given herself to him, but that, in a certain sense, he ceases to respect himself, since he considers himself as perpetually offered to the other. Infidelity signifies that the individual denies his own intimacy in favor of a permanent and quasi-public availability that kills it in its very mystery.

The exclusiveness of fidelity is, undoubtedly, difficult to understand. Against it plays that incessant renewal and transformation of a being who has a history. And this history bears witness that all the individual's other choices are not at all irrevocable. Fidelity implies a renunciation, a sacrifice, a determined will no longer to give to new encounters that the individual might have the same meaning that one special encounter (and why *that* one?) had at one sole time in his life. Has not a mistake been made? Has not one's generosity itself hidden reality? It is impossible, even to faith, to strip this decisive encounter of every element of contingency. A psychological analysis would unveil quite a bit of illusion in it. The person whom I have known (in the Biblical sense of the term " to know," extremely significant in the light of what we have just said) — was she truly the one with whom my life could blossom forth? Such a question never brings an entirely satisfactory reply.

Let us try, however, in continuing with the preceding line of thought, to understand what sexual love (which, because it is sexual, is also personal love) requires as its necessary complement of exclusiveness.

One thought in particular seems instructive. It is aimed not at love itself but at all forms of human relationships. All human relationships are selective. When they are not, they sink into banality. This banality means that all beings have become equal and interchangeable. It is undoubtedly good that one can be attracted by the humanity of each being and that all human relationships are, in principle, stamped with a sort of benevolent urbanity and attractiveness which are codified and institutionalized by the rules of good manners. It is also good that the relationships of the man with all women carry that quiet homage to their femininity which we call courtesy, indeed gallantry. But what would a human being be who remained only on this level, whose relationships with his fellow beings were marked only by the necessary respect of politeness?

On the basis of this refined and civil life we can isolate certain elective and selective affinities. Now, the mark of every elective relationship is that it is at the same time exclusive. It can have depth only at this price. One cannot be the friend of everyone. We would justly mistrust the quality of a friendship that would be distributed without choice, that is, without exclusiveness. True friendships, those which not only resist all the tests of life but are expressed in generosity and trust, are rare. Fidelity in friendship means that one's word has been given to another, a word that can no longer be taken back or shared. Fidelity is the gift of something unique: one's word, one's good word.

For even greater reason, complete love (for example, that which I devote to my children) cannot be shared. It cannot be transferred to others who would merit it and who, in reality perhaps, would merit it even more. But for even greater reason yet, that final form of human love which is sexual love (love where the intimacy of the other and of oneself reveal themselves to each other) requires an absolute exclusiveness. Passion encourages this exclusiveness, but it is incapable of stubbornly defending it. Even the inconstant man has an inkling of this exclusiveness. He is incapable of loving more than one woman at a time. He knows that his love would not be true if it were not accompanied by an oath of fidelity and if, at the time of this oath, he were not of good faith.

All these remarks are located on the plane of psychology and intersubjective experience. Even though they give a sufficient justification to the institution of monogamy and remove its character as a contingency of civilization, they still cannot persuade us that sexual love must normally have the nature of an irrevocable giving. Persons change profoundly in the course of their life. Why should love follow these changes?

As Otto Piper has clearly shown, the mystery of the sexual life could not be truly understood apart from the intended purpose of man as Scripture reveals it to us. Scripture, indeed, far from limiting sexuality to the fulfillment of a biological function, shows us that it is tied to a knowledge of ourselves and of the other: " Both knowledge of the unity of the partners and awareness of the differences between the sexes are implied in the mystery of sex. The assurance that in spite of their strangeness they have merged into unity gives the partners a feeling of happiness. . . . The sexual differentiation may become the cause of hatred between the sexes, because the individual in being so terribly proud to be a Self resents the loss of his (or her) ability to lead an independent life." [77] Sexual relations abolish the distances between the sexes that biological and psychological individuality make us accept as absolutes. The married couple form one sole flesh; in Biblical language this term " flesh " designates, in this respect, a personal unity: " They are no longer two, but one." And in this unity there is a divine blessing, which is to reduce the tendency to see the unity only as a sensual delight. This blessing is why man and woman live in expectation of mutual fulfillment precisely on condition that the act of coition be not for each the occasion of an egoistic enjoyment, which would enclose each one in his or her isolation and which would turn their personal relationship into a relationship of subject to object. The immoderateness of the sexual life has, as an inevitable consequence, the deterioration of personal relationships such as we see in Don Juanism and, in the extreme, in prostitution. Love requires fidelity, just as this unity must be respected and preserved, exactly because the sexual relationship gives birth to a new personal unity, richer than that of the constituent individuals. It is enriched from the fact that their contradictions have been surmounted. It is even richer because it will be the expression of a double generosity and of a double reception.

This unity has a value in itself in the Biblical perspective, and it is striking that for Plato the erotic relationship is only the point of departure for a higher knowledge, the lowest degree of an ascending dialectical movement that is presumed to lead us to the love of the good, the beautiful, and the true, as if personal knowledge were not the highest knowledge there is.

From the Biblical viewpoint, because of the discovery of a new personal unity that is transcendent in relation to the individual characteristics that constitute it, all other human relationships, including those which bind us to our parents, are not reduced in value but are placed on a second level. It is because of his wife that a man must leave his father and his mother (Gen. 2:24; Matt. 19:5). Man will attach himself exclusively to his wife, and this tie will be stronger than the tie, no matter how strong, that attaches him to his friends. The latter no longer have quite the same openness in relation to the married friend. It is the sign of a very marked spiritual inferiority in pagan antiquity, as in present-day Islam, that the man belongs to his friends, to public life, and to his children more than he belongs to his wife. This signifies that the sexual relationship is not lived in all its depth and that the wife is considered more as an instrument than as the partner of a personal unity.

The Old Testament has a more reliable appreciation of the authenticity of this personal relationship when it in-

sists on respect for the unity of the flesh that is established
by the first sex act (Ex. 22:16; Deut. 22:28; 22:13-21,
23 ff.). If we considered this sex act only as an experiment,
an initiation, we would prove quite simply that we do not
understand what it is all about. We would disregard this
new being, born in a reciprocal generosity. But this unity
does not depend solely on our will to constitute it. It is an
objective fact that goes beyond our egoistic intentions and
our frivolity. This is why Paul did not hesitate to say to
the Corinthians, who interpreted Christian liberty as the
possibility of surrendering themselves to all types of sexual
adventures: " You surely know that anyone who links himself with a harlot becomes physically one with her (for
Scripture says, 'The pair shall become one flesh') " (I.
Cor. 6:16, NEB). The relationship with the prostitute is
not sought as a personal relationship, and yet it creates,
whether or not we are aware of it, a unity that will dominate and mark us. Does this mean, then, that fornication
would be a deadly sin, more serious than cowardice or
avarice? In a certain sense yes, because sexual wanton-
ness involves the individual beyond the point where he
means to involve himself, and it also involves the other
person. This is why the apostle can conclude: "Shun fornication. Every other sin that a man can commit is outside
the body; but the fornicator sins against his own body "
(I Cor. 6:18, NEB). The sin consists not only in treating
the person of the other as a means, but also one's own person, since fornication makes use of one's person as if it
were independent, that is, as if it had no intended purpose
and no vocation at all. Paul links in extremely narrow fashion that body which is the source of sexual activity and
that body which belongs to God: " Do you not know that
your body is a shrine of the indwelling Holy Spirit, and

the Spirit is God's gift to you? You do not belong to yourselves " (Ch. 6:19, NEB). Let us not hesitate to correct the
teaching of the apostle, not at all in the name of our own
wisdom, but in the name of the apostolic teaching itself:
other sins are as serious as fornication, carrying with them
a kind of debasement of the person and of the other. They
are a prostitution of the self. Falsehood is undoubtedly
among this number. Yet it is nonetheless true that fornication remains as one of the most glaring forms of contempt
for the other and for the self.

It is precisely because the sexual relationship is a relationship of mutual *belonging*, and that this belonging
gives birth to a new personal unity, that it could not involve several partners. For, inevitably, this repetition
would end by turning the sex act into an act that is sought
for itself, in a sort of ignoring of the person as such and in
the forgetting of the belonging thus created. The libertine
is right whenever he speaks of his sexual adventures as a
type of amusement or pastime, that is, as the opposite of a
commitment. They are for him only the opportunity to obtain some petty vanity from his success, that is, he attaches
little importance to his partner.

But such is the mystery of the sexual life that it ties us
and affects us beyond the feelings and emotions that it
leads us to experience. If there is a metaphysic and a theology of sexuality, it is precisely because it involves us in
an existence in which our motives and conscious intentions are bypassed. We have the illusion that we are absolute masters of our actions and that our actions have no
other meaning than that which we give to them. In reality,
this description fits only our technical activities; in each
specifically human act there is an interrelationship between the person initiating the action and the action it-

self. The action becomes a part of the acting person; man and woman, in the sexual encounter, are overtaken in their conscious or unconscious intentions. This is what Scripture means when it speaks to us of this new flesh to which man and woman, without having wished it, have given birth. The child that can be born from their encounter is only the objective realization of that beyond themselves which they have unveiled.

What we have just said regarding the sexual involvement could, moreover, be repeated for all other forms of human fidelity. In giving his word to someone, the individual is transferred beyond that which he had desired. But his word has been given, a yes has been pronounced that leads his individual liberty to be compromised under forms that he had not foreseen and that he was incapable of foreseeing. But in the sex act he pronounces an even more decisive yes, one that mortgages the future even more, because it is the yes not of one's calculating intellect but of one's incarnate being, that is, of one's true being.

CHAPTER IX

Marriage and Engagement

T HE PROBLEM of the sexual life is resolved by access to love in fidelity; it is not necessarily resolved by marriage. For there exist, in fact, many types of marriage. There is the marriage that serves the partners (or one of them) only as a form of discipline and restraint, more or less tolerable. There are marriages that constitute simple acquiescence to social conventions and that, consequently, ignore the sexual problem entirely. There are also marriages, although more rare, where the sexual life is consistently repressed and where a laborious and sterile search is pursued for a love falsely called spiritual. The institution of monogamic marriage is not, in itself, a solution to the problem of love. It simply offers a social and legal setting, more favorable than polygamy, for the blossoming of a personal love and for the creation of a receptive household for children. We should not be afraid to speak of the ambiguity of the institution of marriage, where social control is aimed at guaranteeing intimacy and where discipline is aimed at stemming the tumultuous force of Eros. " It is a fact," writes Paul Ricoeur, " that man has attained his humanity and has humanized his sexuality only through the discipline, costly in many respects, of the conjugal institution. . . . Marriage is, in our civilization, always to some degree under the mark of duty. Many people are defeated by it. Marriage can protect the duration and the intimacy of the sexual bond, and therefore render it human. But it can also be what ruins for many both its duration and its intimacy." [78] If marriage does not instruct love and does not permit it to become fidelity, then it is no longer anything but a social institution, just as relative as all the others. It does not hinder, and perhaps even favors, the debasement of love into habit, a debasement that is described with sadness and truth by one of the heroines of a novel by Paul André Lesort: " Even then, when he made me pregnant with this child, we no longer came together except out of habit. Pure habit, a need for going through the motions between us, and no longer anything of ourselves in the motions." [79]

There is no obligatory fidelity. It is more than a duty. This is why marriage leaves room for fidelity without guaranteeing it. There are some marriages that continue out of habit, even with a sort of mutual reliance, without fidelity. Fidelity requires more than a stable environment, more than an honored institution. It is even hostile, in a certain sense, to this stability and immobility. It seeks growth. It wants the joy of mutual assistance and sharing, of common discoveries, and of the building of a common destiny.

Exactly because of the ambiguity of the institution of marriage, Christian thought has endeavored to go beyond the institution in the social sense of the word in order to make a sacrament of it. Protestant theology is rarely involved in this course, or has proposed this solution only with reservations,[80] having, in general, a very narrow definition of sacrament. A sacrament, by definition, is instituted by Christ: it is the mediation, through a symbol, of divine grace concerning our salvation. Marriage, however, even if happy, is not the symbol of our salvation.

The definition of sacrament in Roman Catholic theology is broader, permitting a consideration of different types of sacraments. For Roman Catholic thought, a sacrament is not necessarily related to an event in the historical ministry of Christ. Ever since Thomas Aquinas, the Roman Catholic Church has taught that each sacrament has a form, consisting normally of the sacramental words pronounced by the priest, and a content, which is the tangible object serving as the symbol. This definition applies imperfectly enough to marriage, since the blessing pronounced by the priest does not have sacramental value and the sacrament is administered by the spouses themselves. The form and content of the sacrament is thus contained in the mutual agreement of the spouses. The Lord has elevated to sacramental dignity the legitimate union of man and woman, attaching to this union a grace which sanctifies the conjoints. When a man and a woman, under the conditions prescribed by the Church and knowing that they are obedient to the will of God, decide to unite together in an irrevocable fashion, they consummate the sacrament of marriage.

We do not see any necessity to quibble with Roman Catholic theologians over the fact that their definition of sacrament can be applied only with some difficulty to marriage. For no theology possesses, on the basis of Scriptural witness, a truly satisfactory definition of sacrament in general.

Rather, we think it more useful to consider the intention that is expressed in this attempt to elevate marriage to sacramental dignity.

It is a question, first of all, of recalling that marriage is

willed by God, that his blessing is attached to this bond
which unites man and woman. Through marriage a grace
of God comes to man. Marriage is for his good: in it is
realized the profound goal of man, outside of personal
solitude, in the unity of the couple. Valid in itself, this
unity leads to procreation, which in turn extends mortal
man's power over the future. It permits him to make of
the father-son relationship, which is a decisive experience
of humanity, a relationship with someone other than himself, a relationship in which he even recognizes himself.
Undoubtedly one of the greatest errors of certain philosophical anthropologies is that they have not taken into
account man's calling to paternity: Marxism defines man
through work alone. The account of Genesis, on the other
hand, links procreation and work. And in any event, the
creative aspect of work is, in the final analysis, often only
a pale reflection of the procreative activity of man.

In the second place, since marriage is willed by God
and by grace given to man, it cannot be isolated from the
spiritual destiny of man, that is, from his redemption. We
should be careful to avoid any dissociation between the
natural and the supernatural (which is often found in
Roman Catholicism), between the Order of Creation and
the Order of Redemption. It is in Christ, in the redeeming
Christ and through him, that God has created all things
(Col. 1:16). Nothing authorizes us to think that a temporal
grace is not also a spiritual grace. When the Old Testament speaks of blessings, it is remarkable that earthly happiness and temporal prosperity are implied as well as
eternal life. They are in a constant ambiguity. Nothing
could be more false than to set happiness over against salvation. To be sure, the blessings of the Old Testament do
not have a self-sufficient meaning. They refer to the fulfill-

ment that they proclaim. The benevolence of God, who wishes both happiness and salvation for his creature, appears more clearly when the fulfillment has taken place.

This is why Paul does not hesitate to place side by side the union of Christ with his church and the union of man with woman in marriage. But this parallel has meaning only when referred to the history of salvation. This means simply that marriage does not have redemptive significance by itself. It is ambiguous, and can lead to our ruin as well. Whoever unites himself to a prostitute becomes one flesh with her. As a fornicator, he will not inherit the Kingdom. But whoever is already united by faith to the Lord can, through that alone, sanctify the spouse (I Cor. 7:14).

Therefore the unbelief of one of the conjoints never constitutes a reason for repudiation or divorce. A true union between a Christian and a non-Christian, where Eros is not aberrant but is integrated into a personal communion, can lead the nonbelieving conjoint to discover the source that strengthens the life of the other and, ultimately, of the couple itself. This is understandable even on the psychological or moral level.

Indeed, this is why the church, in principle, should not dread mixed marriages or even forbid them, as does, also in principle, the Roman Catholic Church. To be sure, the churches are right in pointing out very strongly the psychological, moral, and spiritual dangers and difficulties that mixed marriages involve. The delicate and often painful problem of the religious education of the children should also be pointed out. But they should also recall that there is sometimes a promise and a hope bound to mixed marriage, on condition that the believing conjoint has an adult faith.

The institution of marriage acquires its true significance only at the cost of a tie between the Order of Redemption and the Order of Creation, of a tie, therefore, between the love that God has for man and man's own carnal love. i.e., at the cost of Eros being taken in charge by Agape. Marriage does not possess its true significance in and of itself. Certainly, one can give monogamous marriage credit for a certain stability, a discipline of passions, and a greater dignity accorded to woman. But legal and social restraint, although it might stabilize mores, does not create an ethical existence. There always exists a deep heteronomy between the institution of marriage and that which it claims to codify. Fidelity is not at all engendered by discipline. Few examples attest more clearly than fidelity to the reality of what Paul calls the end of the law. This fidelity, to be sure, can be sustained by customs; by the sanctions, however uncertain, of public opinion; by feelings of reliance, esteem, and affection that are born of the common life; by the growing old of Eros; and by a certain lack of imagination and audacity on the part of the married couple. These realities, although humble and equivocal, cannot be scorned; they are very precious supports. But they do not constitute the foundation of marriage. It would be dreadful to see in fidelity only a cooled passion. True fidelity is active and creative. It does not let itself become the prey to habit. On the contrary, it desires to fulfill the other in fulfilling itself. It is the love for the other beyond what the other is at the present time. It is the anticipation of the manifestation of the other.

This is why fidelity has an affinity with faith. It believes that what we are, my spouse and I, has not yet been totally manifested. Thus one can establish a link between God's fidelity in relation to us and conjugal fidelity. The fidelity of God signifies that God shows an incredible patience toward us, looking at us through the promise he has given to us, i.e., he sees us in Jesus Christ. So in the same way conjugal fidelity is faith in that promise which is given to each of the conjoints and to the couple itself. The exchange of promises in the religious marriage should not be considered as the essential fact of the ceremony. For these promises, taken in themselves, constitute an untenable wager: I count on the persistency of my present feelings, I wager against the deteriorations of time, I deceive myself regarding my constancy.

In reality, these promises which are exchanged are against common sense if they are not based on an awareness of God's fidelity toward us. The state, which cannot call forth this fidelity, is quite right in reducing the contents of these obligations and in limiting them to a certain number of mutual services and forms of assistance. And it is also right in not affirming the indissolubility of marriage (which is, however, what the Roman Catholic Church requires of the state in opposing all civil legislation authorizing divorce). When the married couple cannot count on the fidelity of God, their commitments cannot go beyond the limits of what is reasonable. This is to say that a marriage based on fidelity is scarcely possible outside of the church. Within the church the limitations imposed by the marriage law cease to be artificial and intolerable disciplines, and the intimate relationship between man and woman appears as the symbol and the declaration both of the communion and of the liberty of the Kingdom. In saying this, we do not ignore the fact that there are, on the outside of faith, faithful couples whose fidelity is all the more admirable since, to human eyes, it is ignorant of its own foundation. But the existence of such couples should not lead us to put confidence in human possibilities.

It is evident that the idea of making of marriage a sacrament is not devoid of meaning, on the condition, however, that no *opus operatum* is tied to this sacrament, that it is not reduced to a magical-juridical mechanicalism. The error of the Roman Catholic Church consists precisely in making of the marriage sacrament an absolute obstacle to divorce. Most assuredly, it is necessary to condemn divorce resolutely, as Jesus did (Matt. 5:32). But, in fact, divorce is brought about in the same way that infidelity toward God is brought about. As God forgives infidelity toward himself, so the mocked partner forgives the infidelity that comes to him. We cannot insist too much on the power of a forgiveness that is capable of annulling the past. But it also happens sometimes that forgiveness is beyond our measure of faith, or that forgiveness is not received as such and, consequently, does not become an object upon which the forgiven person can begin a new life.[81] There are also breaches that are final. Jesus warns us that "every one who looks at a woman lustfully has already committed adultery with her in his heart" (Matt. 5:28). This adultery certainly does not mean that divorce is the irreparable result, that the course of fidelity is henceforth closed. We should at least understand that fidelity cannot be secured by constraint, no more than faith can. Thus, after all humanly possible attempts at reconciliation have been tried, why should a conjugal union be continued that is already void of meaning and that is no longer anything but hypocrisy? Why continue a relationship that in many cases, through the irritation it provokes, hinders the man or the woman from rediscovering not only a balanced moral life but even access to divine forgiveness, and that can be for the children the cause of a scandal or of psychological troubles?

Although one can legitimately reproach the Protestant churches for sometimes too lightly authorizing the remarriage of divorced persons, thus bringing contempt on the divine blessing, they cannot be reproached for not having made divorce impossible. Divorce is the result of sin. It must be understood as such, and it must also be understood that, in principle, this sin is one of the two partners. But it is impossible for us not to recognize the sin in its social and moral consequences, to act as if these consequences did not exist.

In emphasizing the sacramental significance of marriage, that is, the necessary tie between the fidelity of God and that of the conjoints, and in insisting on the fact that conjugal fidelity is a grace, we do not absolutely prohibit recourse to all forms of human wisdom that can help us remain in this fidelity. Quite the contrary, it is in the certitude that all is grace that we can and must work out our own sanctification. This is why Christians have been quite wrong in depriving themselves of the assistance of Eros and in not maintaining its force. Its presence is necessary in a Christian marriage. And Karl Barth is right in criticizing Anders Nygren for being too eager to combat Eros and to reduce its value, as if Eros were not a part of God's good creation.[82] A Christian marriage is not a marriage of convenience; it is a marriage of love and passion.

In our age it is no longer necessary, happily, to be on guard against that bourgeois idea that would prefer marriage to come later in life (for the man!), as a sign of the abatement or even of the weariness of a previously immoderate sexual life, as if one had reached a time in life when a more settled existence is possible, the sensual life having been satisfied in other ways. On the other hand, our age can, perhaps, find something of value in one minor element of this supposed wisdom of our fathers. Is it not necessary to guard against the hasty marriage that follows after the first spark of love? For this first spark can be purely sentimental and naïve. It can be more the excitement of the young man who discovers with wonder, not the one who will be his wife, but rather *the* Young Woman, and who hastens to marry, not his wife but, in her person, every young woman and all femininity. Eros, in its first phase, is still undifferentiating. It carries the person toward the other sex in general. Imagination colors the first encounter with all possible charms. One will marry then; one will repent afterward. A maturing of Eros is necessary, an initiation of the young person to the other sex. A preliminary generic knowledge must be acquired before choosing and being chosen (the initiative must not be one-way).

This is why it seems wise not to discredit *flirtation,* as Protestant moralism has so often done. The medieval church encouraged gallantry and the chivalrous spirit, which are only stylized forms of flirtation. But it is necessary that both sides know what flirtation is and that no one be fooled by it. They should understand that flirtation is both serious and wonderful, and that it nevertheless remains a game. It must, therefore, be accompanied by humor and by a certain levity, without sentimentality becoming involved in it. Our ancestors, who understood it well, used the happy expression " *conter fleurettes* " [literally, " to recount little flowers," — tr.]. A sort of roundelay, a sort of dance where each sex becomes acquainted with the other, that's flirtation. Consequently, it must not have too secret a character. Although nascent love passes through a period of secretiveness, flirtation is carried on in a collectivity of young men and women. But once again, like all games, flirtation has a set of rules. And the first rule is lucidity. This lucidity is likely to saturate the game with guilt feelings, which can be shaken off only by a complete honesty. Flirtation can prevent marriage from being a manifestation of puerility.

And yet marriage does not presuppose a serious weighing of the future. It is not the result of a calculation in which one puts all the odds on his side after duly making inquiries. It is a great risk to run and it should be run gladly. The joy will be all the greater in proportion as we are not hypnotized by the singular gravity of our commitment. " An individual without a sense of humor," Dr. Bovet says, with humor, " should never get married." [83] It is this humor, which is true only to the extent that it is based on the deep assurance of faith, which will permit a confrontation of the first difficulties of common existence, the first clashes of character and taste, the manifestations of the profound otherness of the partners, without dramatizing them. It is this humor which will stem the envenomed, but quite natural, outbursts of jealousy and will spare love from becoming tyrannical and possessive.

Although it is true that the honeymoon, which is the apprenticeship of life together, requires a certain discretion on the part of the couple's friends, it is not at all true that a happy household is necessarily the one in which each of the conjoints breaks all ties with friends from before the marriage, in which the man and woman renounce, in particular, their friendships among the other sex (such a renouncing can lead to each of the partners reproaching the other later on for having forced the renouncing). There is, undoubtedly, a peril attached to these friendships. But it is necessary to run the risk and at the same time to free one-

self from it by giving no illicit aspect to the friendships.[84]
Marriage is fundamentally an acknowledgment of reciprocal belonging. Through marriage the individual, in
this very acknowledgment, commits the secret of his existence to the care of the partner. He will belong only to
her. Betrayal exists already when one confides to a third
party, of whatever sex, an innermost anxiety, an existential
inquietude that could not be acknowledged to the other
spouse. But, this being said, friends remain a precious
thing, who by their dependable presence preserve the
couple from a sort of psychologically inevitable boredom,
and who, above all, aid the couple to avoid withdrawing
into themselves and to avoid practicing a collective egoism. Friends help the couple to remain open to the calls of
the world, of culture, and of politics. It is conversation
that saves the home, yet this conversation must be given
fullness by preoccupations other than domestic and
culinary ones. It is necessary that the marvelous diversity
of the world find its place in the home and that the dialogue of the married couple be open to others. The hospitality of the home is one of the conditions for its health.

To be sure, this health is preserved only insofar as the
home is not undermined by its own friends and insofar as
the hospitality does not become a whirl of social relationships with the many " obligations " that such sociability involves. For then the invasion of the home by friends and
its involvement in external relationships would mean that
the couple cannot endure their own privacy, that it has
become meaningless for them. And soon they will attempt
to have their own individual relationships outside the
home, to give to these relationships an aspect of private
domain.

Even when this peril is overcome, when the couple
themselves assume the many worldly relationships that

are often the result of the social or socioprofessional situation, it is advisable carefully to watch that the home does not become a sort of extension of the professional life. Just as it would be false for the husband not to keep his wife abreast of his professional problems (largely the case in the middle class of the nineteenth century), so it would be false to turn the home into a place for professional appointments. It would be wrong to value the home only for the conveniences that it offers for transacting business and for fostering good relationships with clients and colleagues.[85] It should be remembered in this respect that if society is not the extension of the family, neither is the family the extension of society. The family is the particular society entrusted with the guardianship of private life.

Whether or not it will remain this will depend obviously on the individuality of the conjoints. It is the absence of individuality in one of the partners (or sometimes in both) that creates rapidly and permanently that particular type of boredom peculiar to the family. The call to others then becomes a compensation for this boredom. To be sure, it is exceptional when both partners have the same degree or the same type of individuality. In a couple there is nearly always a dominant element. It becomes serious when the dominant element, in asserting his (or her) superiority too strongly, becomes destructive of the other, when, for example, the wife is reduced to the function of admiring her husband. The husband undoubtedly will be pleased by this, but only for a certain time. The admiration that his spouse has for him, and that perhaps she alone has for him, will profoundly bore him. On the other hand, a wife who exercises a perpetually critical function toward her husband will produce in him, besides discouragement and various types of inferiority complexes, an irritated boredom.

Although it is true that a couple, because the members are one flesh, must have its own personality, this can only give birth to the development of the personality of the partners: there must be, in the couple, a sort of mutual development, each one having clearly marked the potentialities in the other and, where possible, the particular calling of the other. This calling underlines the particularity and the limitations of the other partner. It is necessary that each of the spouses has ambitions for the other that are compatible with his calling and limitations. Many conjugal disappointments derive from the fact that one of the conjoints has excessive ambitions for the other, which secretly makes him grieve over his inability to realize them. This is to say that there will be mutual development only where the partners are first of all accepted for what they are, with the very limitations of their particular vocation. The dictum "Accept your spouse as he or she is" would be equivocal if it meant a renunciation of any progress. But we can be allowed to wish for this progress only in the direction compatible with a character and a vocation. If I am by nature a conscientious and intelligent subordinate, and not one who takes bold initiatives, my wife must not require me to become a leader. Such a requirement would be disastrous and would leave feelings of resentment and disappointment in the hearts of both. The man and wife must not settle down into a routine life, but they must be encouraged with prudence and discernment to acquire more authority and more prestige in the realm that is their own. The concern for social promotion must not be the principal ambition of the couple. The happiness of the home can be destroyed by the very demands of a civilization of work that, in the near future, will have less and less need of inferior workers and will exercise a very strong pressure for social promotion.

There is a form of acceptance of the other that is particularly difficult in the couple: this is the acceptance of the other in his growing old. We say intentionally the aging of the other; for although the acceptance of our own growing old is sometimes quite facilitated by nature (which proportions our energies and our ambitions to our strength and our age) and encouraged both by the growing old of our contemporaries and by a sort of fatalism as old as humanity, we accept with more difficulty the aging of our spouse. The difficulty seems to be the greatest for man, who stupidly would like his wife to remain always young.[86] This ambition is not completely puerile, since it expresses the obscure awareness of a Biblical teaching, viz., that the woman is the glory of her husband. Rather, the puerility consists in not having perceived that the wife is this glory in all the ages of life, in not being attentive to the special charm of youth, to that of young adulthood, to that of maturity, and to that of middle age. The frequency of divorces that come after fifteen or twenty years of marriage is the statistical expression of this type of resentment which some conjoints nourish toward the other because the other grows old.

It is certain that the acceptance of the growing old of the other presupposes something different from resignation and fatalism. It presupposes the sort of faith by which one can discern in the person of the other a reality different from that which is shaped and sometimes disfigured by time, the subject upon whom the divine promise is pronounced, the new being whose existence is attested by baptism. This requirement that we accept the growing old of others is valid for all our interpersonal relationships. How much more reason is there, then, to accept it in the husband-wife relationship, the exemplary relationship of all human relationships!

The growth of the personality of each partner in the bosom of the conjugal union is subordinated to a condition that is both psychological and moral: it is necessary that each of the partners escape from the influence of his own family and that he free himself from the emotional fixations inherited from early childhood.[87]

We should admire the wisdom of the redactor of Genesis, who could not be supposed to have had a knowledge of the secrets of depth psychology, yet who nonetheless has given this fundamental rule: " Therefore a man leaves his father and his mother and cleaves to his wife " (Gen. 2:24). It is necessary to insist on the physical sense of this verb " to leave." The concern of our modern societies should be to give to each young couple housing that is *theirs*, where they can live in independence from the parents. But this physical break should be accompanied by a psychological break as well. This is the price of reaching adulthood. Not only should the home be able to make its decisions without assistance (even if it includes the advice of preceding generations), but the husband and wife should belong to each other more than they belong to their parents. The man who remains too much a son will not be a true husband and he should not consider his wife as a new mother. The question is even more delicate since, psychologically, conjugal love is not always dissociated from paternal love and maternal love. Many men treat their wives as children. The protection that is given to the wife takes on the air of paternalism, and the wife, in turn, especially when she is childless, envelops her husband in an anxious and possessive love that does not permit him to assume the risks of life and to take the initiatives of an adult. The spouses love each other and yet are "poorly loved" (François Mauriac). And their love will curiously develop into resentment, each one reproaching the other for not having permitted him (or her) to become an adult.

Much healthy stress is put on the continuity that the family, through the forming of a lineage, introduces into the midst of society. This is undoubtedly an essential aspect of its function. But it is necessary to see that the family also creates a discontinuity. It forms cells that are separated in time, groups that do not reproduce each other exactly in the course of generations. Thus it breaks traditions at the same time that it maintains certain others, thereby participating in the necessary renewal of humanity.

The fulfillment of the couple, the fulfillment of the conjoints in the interior of the couple, constitutes an essential activity of humanity, which is something we too often forget in a civilization of work. It is a slow task that is never totally finished, not even in the evening of life. It requires unceasing renewals, but it is also the assurance, for the couple, that it truly has a future before it, even when it has finished the education of its children, which sounds for it the hour of retirement.

ENGAGEMENT

We could certainly have spoken of engagement at the time of dealing with flirtation. The occurrence of engagement emerges sometimes slowly or suddenly out of a period of flirtation. But flirtation and engagement are far from having the same meaning or the same finality. Flirtation is that game of love by which young men and women acquire a mutual knowledge, a generic knowledge. An engagement no longer belongs to the realm of games. It involves a choice and a form of commitment. And it should, in the normal course of events, lead to marriage. If we speak of engagement after having spoken of marriage, it is because its meaning is defined by that of marriage. The engagement is a promise of marriage, but not a trial marriage.

The status of engagements is paradoxical enough. The fiancés are not husband and wife, although their reciprocal fidelity can be as great as that which binds husbands and wives. They know that they must wait, that it would not be good for them, having chosen each other, to be man and wife right off. They know that it would not be good for their first encounter to be a sexual encounter, for then they would give a kind of priority and primacy to the inclination that is undoubtedly present and that has attracted them to each other, but that should submit to a maturation. It should become filled with friendship, tenderness, and psychological and spiritual understanding before being able to exert itself, precisely in order to lessen the risk of it becoming aberrant.

On the other hand, it is neither necessary nor desirable for the engagement period to be very long, as has been the case in the past. If the engagement period is a time of expectation, this expectation, when it is prolonged for too great a time, risks uselessly intensifying the desire. It is a time truly unique in human existence. It is the time of the promise, where what will be us is already mysteriously given under the form of a promise — and where, at the same time, nothing irrevocable is yet completed. Although the engagement is not a trial marriage, it should, however, be a period of testing in which the fiancés verify the authenticity of their feelings, the soundness of their choice, and in which they have a glimpse of each other not only as individuals but as representatives of a certain family tradition, of a certain social milieu. In an age where the barriers of social class undoubtedly play a more effaced role in the choice of a mate than in the past, the engagement period takes on a special importance. For it is an illusion to think that one marries solely an individual being, that it is possible to disregard the social and intellectual milieu of which this individual, whether he knows it or not, is the representative.

To say that the engagement period is a time of testing is to imply that there is a possibility that the result of the testing can be negative, and that the engagement can be broken. Protestant moralism has often encumbered engagements with an excessive seriousness, considering their ruptures as being as grave and as degrading as a divorce. This is a prejudice that destroys the true meaning of engagements. Certainly, a commitment is involved in the engagement that, as such, is not conditional, and the breach of this commitment is painful, all the more so because it is very rarely the doing of both fiancés at once. It will leave one of them, if not both, the memory of a broken communion, of an impossible love, impossible because not shared, of a love offered and not received. Now, it is the essence of love to be shared; it is not wrong to speak of an unhappy love, when it is unrequited. But it is sometimes the proof of an authentic courage, of a true honesty, of a true faith (God should not be tempted by asking him to sustain us in an experience that is beyond our forces), to break off an engagement that does not promise happiness, to break it off with simplicity in the hope that a true friendship, sincere and affectionate, can one day be reborn.

Yet in order for this to be possible it is necessary for the engagement not to have been encumbered with too great an air of solemnity. Middle-class society gives quite readily, but wrongly, a publicity to engagements that is a bit too noisy, thus prejudging the future. Inversely, secret engagements are not to be recommended; it is good for the fiancés to know themselves committed to each other from a certain moment, and that their friends respect with discretion their privacy. It will be invaluable help to the fiancés not to know themselves engaged only in the secrecy of the heart, but of being recognized as such in the circles in which they run. There is a middle ground between premature solemnity and uncertain clandestineness.

Modern psychologists rightly insist on the fact that the harmony between a man and a woman is not only of the feelings and of spiritualized affectivity. There is, more deeply, a sort of sexual assent. In this semiconscious realm certain irremediable incompatibilities can exist despite feelings. Moreover, it is certain that the sexual life of the man follows a rhythm different from that of the woman. In the woman, frigidity is frequently the mark of a sexual incompatibility that is difficult to overcome. Is this a motive for transforming the engagement period into a trial marriage? Many psychologists and physicians are of this opinion. But the proposed remedy seems to us to be quite dubious, and worse than the danger run: the end result would be to give a primary place to sexual Eros and to consider it in and of itself as animal function; whereas when it is integrated into the person and colored with tender affection, it is capable of evolving and even of changing.

On the other hand, this suggestion would deprive marriage of its fundamental quality: it would no longer be an absolute beginning in our life, the entry into a new existence. In the full sense of the term, one would deflower it. Also, without disregarding the risks pointed out by psychologists and physicians (risks that should be explained in " schools of preparation for marriage "; for in this area explanation can liberate), it is advisable to remember that as act and wager of fidelity, marriage necessarily involves certain risks, and that marriage could not fall to the level of a reasonable calculation without losing that which gives it its dignity and its charm, its character of human adventure, the greatest adventure that it is given to man to run.

CHAPTER X

Celibacy

WE HAVE CONSIDERED marriage as the fulfillment of man in the community of the couple, as access to authentic maturity, and as the realization of the merciful will of God toward man. We have spoken also of conjugal fidelity, in which man expresses his obedience to the faithful God. All these arguments do not seem to leave an important place for celibacy. Should we then conclude, as does the Old Testament, that celibacy is only a sort of exception, of abnormality, and of unhappiness?

We have been careful not to forget that a large number of unmarried men and women who have not chosen the state of celibacy have perfectly succeeded in giving, especially through their professional activity, a personal radiance and a fullness and harmony to their existence that many couples have not achieved. But it is incontestable that celibacy is often an unhappiness. The number of women is greatly superior to that of men. This has resulted, by mathematical necessity, in the fact that many women who have wanted to marry, who have seriously envisaged marriage, are forced to forgo it. This renouncing is difficult because the solitary life is a hardship and a temptation, because celibacy, although it releases one from numerous responsibilities and numerous sacrifices, deprives a person of the joy of a shared life, of a life given and recovered in the person of the partner and of the children.

One of the most painful aspects of celibacy is that type of segregation which exists between couples and single persons. The couples invite only other couples into their homes. When an unmarried person joins these groups he often feels unwanted. The loneliness of the single person follows him. To be sure, the church thinks of the unmarried persons in the community, but it usually wants to use them, to profit from their availability by entrusting responsibilities to them. This is undoubtedly good, because in doing this the church helps the unmarried to discover the meaning of their single state. Indeed, it need not be admitted that a phenomenon, determined and foreseeable by the application of a probability calculus, is *ipso facto* devoid of meaning and cannot be the bearer of an authentic vocation. It would be a quite romantic conception of vocation to consider that it is always discovered in the first burst of enthusiasm, in a complete freedom. The most reliable callings are born from reflecting on a situation that is more or less imposed on us. A vocation is nearly always a way of accepting a situation that was first of all considered as a limitation. The church must, therefore, help unmarried persons to assume their situation, to discover the meaning of it, and to understand that although God has not allowed them certain joys and certain responsibilities, he has reserved others for them. The church must aid them to see that the solitude of the unmarried state can be relative, that the unmarried person, precisely because he does not have family obligations, can be father or mother to all those who do not have real parents or can extend the influence of parents in certain directions.

It is not by chance that the teaching or educative career includes a relatively high number of single persons. There is a moral and intellectual parturition that is not always the privilege of those who give birth carnally. There is also a spiritual parturition that permitted the apostles to speak to the faithful as to their children. To lead a being not solely toward adulthood but toward the act of faith, to lead him mysteriously toward this act through the witness that one presents to him, is truly to give birth. Ancient Israel, as we have seen, considered the perpetuation of the race as the duty essential to its election. For this reason Israel did everything to avoid celibacy. But the New Israel, the People of God, recruits not by filiation according to the flesh, but by spiritual begetting. It is in this sense that the church can be called Mother, and it should join very closely to its ministry those who are deprived of family.

Yet the church should also be occupied with promoting the insertion of unmarried persons into families or groups of families. This is undoubtedly a delicate task and one not without risks, but it is an imperative task nonetheless, since it is the obligation of the parish to form a sort of family. It should do this not merely by convoking so-called family gatherings, but by bringing into existence, spiritually, a network of families, and integrating the single persons into these families. The present tendency in the church is to group the members of the congregation by age categories or by sociofamilial categories (junior high, senior high, young couples, married women, etc.). This effort, which is far from being devoid of sense, should be balanced by an effort to form properly family-type groups into which the isolated persons can find their places.

However difficult might be the problems posed by *de*

facto celibacy (to give it meaning and to break the solitude of the unmarried person's condition), those problems
posed by freely chosen celibacy are no less formidable.

First of all, it is proper to demythologize the form of
celibacy that is chosen and received as a religious vocation. The reason why this is necessary is that we have behind us a long tradition which sees in celibacy the Christian state par excellence. The celibacy of priests is the
most evident manifestation of this myth which has an ancient source in the consideration of sexuality as culpability.
There is an incompatibility between the sacred and the
profane, between the religious life and marriage. This idea
appeared very early in the history of Christianity, as witness the text from Athenagoras (*Petition on behalf of the
Christians,* written about 177 A.D.): "There are to be
found among us many men and women who have grown
old without marrying, in the hope of belonging more completely to God. If perseverance and voluntary celibacy
bring us near to God, and if the mere thought, the mere
desire of pleasure take us away from him, how much
more should we avoid the acts from whose very thought
we flee." [88] This type of thinking is by no means isolated in the church fathers. Certainly none of them condemn marriage, but many of them tend to regard chastity as a mark of a more eminent Christian life. As early
as the second century there developed in the early church
the idea that the best among the Christians should submit to the exclusive rules of ascetism and, among these
rules, that of celibacy or, for those who were married,
abstention from all sexual relations. The rule of the celibacy of bishops was also settled as early as the second
century, and in the course of the fourth century the
councils progressively made this rule obligatory for all

the degrees of the priesthood, including deacon and sub-deacon. The development of monasticism, which arose as a form of exemplary Christian life, was to have as a result the manifestation of the eminent worth of celibacy.

In the course of this whole evolution, increasingly definite form was given to the idea (whose roots are more Hellenistic than Hebrew) that all service to God is incompatible with the state of marriage. This was particularly true of the service of the altar. The Roman Catholic Church attaches considerable worth to the rule of the celibacy of priests. It is beyond all doubt that one of the reasons why the Roman Catholic Church reacted with such severity toward the worker-priests is that the worker-priest had the ambition to live in the world as a layman and that he had had, short-termed, the idea of getting married.

The Reformation reacted very strongly both against monasticism and against celibacy. Luther's fury against monasticism is well-known. The Augsburg Confession (Article XXIII) argues in favor of the marriage of pastors. It takes its stand both on the general commandment of God (Gen. 1:27-28) and on the counsels of Paul (I Cor. 7:2, 8). It argues by showing that imposed celibacy can lead only to immorality and hypocrisy. The Confession is undoubtedly wrong in presenting marriage as a sort of guarantee against immorality: "God himself . . . has instituted the state of marriage in order to come to the aid of human frailty and in order to hinder immorality." The arguments are far from being decisive, for they reduce marriage to the level of simple means and they risk making celibacy appear as the royal way that is offered to the strong in the faith. The state of monastic morals explains the reaction of the Reformation.

To demythologize celibacy is to pose two principles: first of all, abstention regarding sexual relations does not introduce man into a state of particular holiness, for if the sexual life bears the mark of sin and if egoism is given free play there, it is not more gravely marked with the stamp of sin than other aspects of our existence. Also, celibacy must in no way be considered as the ideal type of Christian life.

In the second place, it is necessary to reject firmly the idea that sexual abstention would be the condition for the exercise of every Christian ministry and, in particular, of the service of the altar, for this would lower the ministry to the role of the manipulation of sacred things and to submit it to the pagan law of the contradistinction of sacred and profane.

Certainly, the apostle Paul writes to the Corinthians, who had consulted him on the question of marriage and celibacy, and on the renouncing by married couples of all sexual relations: " Do not refuse one another except perhaps by agreement for a season, that you may devote yourselves to prayer; but then come together again, lest Satan tempt you through lack of self-control " (I Cor. 7:5). But this is nothing other than a general principle of moderation. Common sense should remind man that there is a time for such a thing.

After the demythologizing of celibacy has been completed, it remains that Paul, contrary to the Reformation, did indeed counsel the nonmarried Christians to remain in the state of celibacy: " To the unmarried and the widows I say that it is well for them to remain single as I do. But if they cannot exercise self-control, they should marry. For it is better to marry than to be aflame with passion " (I Cor. 7:8-9). He had even put at the beginning of his development a sort of principle: "It is well for a man not to touch a woman" (v. 1). To the fathers who give their daughters in marriage, the apostle declares that they do well, but that they do better still if they do not give their daughters in marriage (vs. 37-38).[89]

It is evident that although the apostle Paul had no objections to marriage, even considering it essential for some people, celibacy seemed preferable to him. The various Christian sects that have made an ideal of celibacy will always find in Paul a serious Scriptural support.

However, it should be noted that Paul took great care to emphasize the relativity of his counsels. There is a vocation of marriage and a vocation of celibacy: "I wish that all were as I myself am. But each has his own special gift from God, one of one kind and one of another" (v. 7). Even more, the apostle himself stressed that although he speaks with the authority of the Lord when it is a question of forbidding divorce and repudiation (vs. 10-11), when it is a question of recommending celibacy he speaks in his own name: "Now concerning the unmarried, I have no command of the Lord. But I give my opinion as one who by the Lord's mercy is trustworthy" (v. 25). And, at the end of the chapter, Paul comes once again to the fact that the counsels he gives are counsels of expediency given by a man who, to be sure, has received the Holy Spirit of God, but who speaks nevertheless under his own responsibility. After having called to mind that the widow is free to remarry, "only in the Lord" (which means undoubtedly that she should marry a Christian), he adds: "But in my judgment she is happier if she remains as she is. And I think that I have the Spirit of God" (vs. 39-40).

Let us go one step farther: what is the basic motivation for these counsels? In Paul's eyes the Parousia is near: "I

mean, brethren, the appointed time has grown very short "
(v. 29). Therefore it scarcely makes any sense to proceed
with human projects. This is the source of the general rule
laid down by Paul: " Only, let everyone lead the life which
the Lord has assigned to him, and in which God has called
him " (v. 17). The wisdom for an eschatological age is to
remain in the state in which one finds oneself. It should
be emphasized that this wisdom does not apply only to the
condition of married persons and single persons. It applies
to the uncircumcised and the circumcised, to slaves and to
free men. To all, the apostle declares: " So, brethren, in
whatever state each was called, there let him remain with
God " (v. 24). A change of state has no meaning at all in
the perspective of the imminence of the Kingdom. It is
proper that each put to profit the condition in which he
finds himself: let the slave know that he is a slave of Christ
(v. 22). In the same way, the single person should remain
unmarried, in order not to bring new concerns on himself
unnecessarily. To get married is, inevitably, to take a
greater part in the concerns of the world, to be no longer
devoted solely to the concern of being pleasing to the
Lord. The intention of the apostle is clear: " I want you to
be free from all anxieties " (v. 32).

Paul's ethic is, therefore, strictly subordinated to his
eschatological vision, to the idea that the generation will
not pass away without the return of Christ being produced. Now, the apostle himself was brought to revise
this vision. He understood that this imminence of the
Parousia, though it was reality, did not necessarily have
the sense of a temporal immediacy. Consequently, the
rule according to which each one should remain in the
civil and social state where he was at the moment of his
conversion loses some of its validity. Who would venture

to assert that it is proper to renounce all efforts for social liberation because of the coming of the Kingdom? Is it not, on the contrary, exactly because of the coming of the Kingdom and as a sign of the seriousness of our expectation that we ought to do all we can to turn the social order upside down in its injustice? If we consider today that because of the total renewal promised by the Kingdom it is worth the trouble to devote all our efforts to bring about the disappearance of all forms of social slavery, we can no longer maintain that the proximity of the Kingdom makes obedience to God's commandments concerning marriage and procreation useless.

This does not mean that the Pauline ethic, as an interim ethic, has lost all value. It is not the thesis of the proximity of the Kingdom that is false. It is simply the manner in which the apostle, in this period of his ministry, conceived the realization of the Kingdom. This ethic, which makes all the world's values relative, including marriage, can be readopted in its entirety: "I mean, brethren, the appointed time has grown very short; from now on, let those who have wives live as though they had none, and those who mourn as though they were not mourning, and those who rejoice as though they were not rejoicing, and those who buy as though they had no goods, and those who deal with the world as though they had no dealings with it. For the form of this world is passing away" (I Cor. 7:29-31).

All Christian marriage ethics should be placed in this eschatological perspective. However important the building of a home may be, this cannot take an absolute value in our eyes, no more than our social advancing. All the values that belong to the times of the present creation — and marriage is one of them — are affected by a coefficient of relativity.

But what is true of marriage must also apply to celibacy. Celibacy certainly represents a possible type of commitment. Yet it cannot boast of a special privilege. Although it is a form of particular availability, it also has its bondage and its limitations. The voluntary celibate ought to know that he avoids a common rule that God has appointed for the good of man and that his attitude can base its authority only on the fulfillment of a special task that requires of him not a special dignity but a more complete availability. Certain forms of Christian ministry can require this availability. It is not at all certain to us that mere cenobitism can require and justify celibacy. Cenobitism certainly bases its authority on a very strong Christian tradition, and its role in the revival of the church is undisputed, but it is not necessarily linked to the existence of the church.

In any case, we do not think that one can write, as does Max Thurian, affirming the superiority of celibacy over marriage, despite the fact that he is a celibate: " Celibacy is a sign of the resurrection and of the coming kingdom of God, because at the resurrection and in the kingdom there is neither marriage nor giving in marriage. In the Church celibacy is thus a reminder of the new order of the Gospel, whereas marriage is still a witness to the old order." [90] This exegesis of Luke 20:34-36 seems to us inadmissible. Jesus, in his reply to the Sadducees who had asked him which of the seven successive husbands of a woman would be her spouse in the future life, declares: " The sons of this age marry and are given in marriage; but those who are accounted worthy to attain to that age and to the resurrection from the dead neither marry nor are given in marriage, for they cannot die any more, because they are equal to angels and are sons of God, being sons of the resurrection " (Luke 20:34-36). Verse 36 shows quite well that the intention of Jesus is to point out that there is no common measure between the life of the age to come and the present age. His intention is not at all to make celibacy a symbol of the resurrection and to link election with celibacy.

Just as it seems unauthorized to want to judge celibacy, so it seems to us to be false for it to set itself up as the bearer of a special religious meaning. Married love, enlightened by the light of the love of Christ for his church, announces as well as celibacy the new love of the Kingdom. Max Thurian writes again: "While we wait for the return of Christ which will give us holiness, we have to live in the world; and, to signify and make real that expectation, we must accept sacrifice, renunciation, discipline, and asceticism into our life.

"Celibacy is one of the signs that remind us of the absolute demands of Christ, of his liberating return, of the establishing of the kingdom of heaven, and of the need to be watchful, to renounce the world, the flesh and covetous desires, and to welcome joyfully in our hearts the sacrifice of our passions in pure love for Jesus." [91] We are fully in accord with Max Thurian on the necessity of renunciation as a symbol of the waiting. But could not one find in marriage all that he rightly finds in celibacy as a sign of this waiting? Is not the devotion of a man to his wife also sacrifice, and is not fidelity sacrifice? Does not the education of children signify renunciation? Max Thurian, again, has written a curious enough statement. He says that celibacy has the property of calling to mind "that Christian marriage, too, includes the demand for sacrifice." We cannot figure out why celibacy would have this property. We must accept the evidence: no human life, however unadorned it might be, constitutes by itself a total sacrifice, an absolute renunciation. But every type of life lived conscientiously in obedience and expectation necessarily bears signs of the Kingdom. These signs are always imperfect and ambiguous, and it is futile to want to establish a hierarchy among them.

It is normal and proper that there be celibates by vocation; this would be only for the purpose of reminding those who are celibates by necessity that their situation is not a misfortune and that it is possible to give to this type of existence a real fullness, that this fullness is discovered especially in the service of the neighbor in the bosom of the community of the church. It is proper and normal to show celibacy in a favorable light, as Karl Barth [92] and, following him, Max Thurian, has done, to show that it truly represents a possibility for man. But it becomes hazardous to insist on presenting this way, this possibility, as a special sign, ultimately superior to all the others, of the expectation of the Kingdom. Certainly, the brothers of Taizé,[93] taking into account the tradition of Protestant ethics that has favored marriage too much, are right in wishing to justify celibacy. But it is with great difficulty that they keep from going beyond this objective and running counter to the ethic of the Reformation.

It is difficult, it seems to us, to argue from the celibacy of Jesus. His mission, let us remember, was comparable to no other mission of man. The only point that one can retain is that Jesus reminds us, by his very existence, that a full humanity is perfectly compatible with celibacy, but for this to be so it is necessary that celibacy be tied to the fulfillment of a particular task.

This is why, in our opinion, Christian ethics must maintain very strictly that marriage is the more regular vocation for man (just like work) and that celibacy, when voluntary, is always an exceptional vocation which will always become connected with different types of conscientious objections and will never justify itself as the " normal state." It is exactly because celibacy was tied to the monastic state that the Reformation so harshly and justly criticized it. The teaching of Jesus remains enigmatic, no doubt on purpose. It is too often forgotten that Jesus gave his teaching on celibacy only after having spoken of the indissolubility of marriage (Matt. 19:1-9). Marriage then appeared to his disciples as a sort of unbearable yoke: " If such is the case of a man with his wife, it is not expedient to marry " (v. 10). They wanted to see in celibacy a more accommodating rule. This is why Jesus replied by emphasizing the exceptional character of celibacy, by insisting on the fact that it is really necessary to have great reasons for committing oneself to this way. This is why he speaks mysteriously of those "eunuchs who have made themselves eunuchs for the sake of the kingdom of heaven" (v. 12). Let him receive this who can, he adds, in order to underline that there is something exceptional in this commitment.

Celibacy is assuredly a way possible for man. But no less assuredly, it is an exceptional way. No special vocation entitles whoever follows it to obtain glory from it.

CHAPTER XI

The Problem of Birth Control

THE COMING of children is the fulfillment of the couple's wish. Yet there exists a problem of the control or of the limitation of births, or as we say, "family planning." This problem, to be sure, has first of all, in our present world, a demographic and social aspect: the growth of the demographic curve takes on a catastrophic character for certain countries, especially the underdeveloped ones. This does not mean that Malthus was absolutely right and that we now have proof that worldwide production could not increase at the same tempo as the population. The only valid affirmation is that in the present economic demographic state of the planet, a situation that is complicated by political tensions and the division of the world into two blocs incapable of cooperating, the problem of hunger could not be resolved. In proportion as the gap grows between the underdeveloped countries and the industrialized countries where abundance reigns, the birthrate will increase in the former, for it is prosperity that constitutes a natural curb on fecundity.

But we are not concerned with this general problem in the context of this chapter. We will deal solely with birth control in relation to the life of the couple and the family.

We have insisted on the fact that the sexual life must be

integrated into the intersubjective life of the married couple and must not be merely the uncontrolled expression of an animal need. The sex act must be the manifestation of a love and of a tenderness. This is to say that it has its finality in itself and that it is not subordinated to the single interest of the perpetuation and the growth of the species. This is to say that it preserves its meaning and its validity outside of the will to procreate. Certainly, as Fr. Marc Oraison has said: " To have sexual relations means to bring into play together the biological power of reproduction, that is, to have children." [94] A deliberate wish to have sexual relations while at the same time systematically refusing the coming of children would attest that one seeks in sexual relations only an egoistic pleasure. It would mean that one has not understood the promise and the blessing linked to the conjugal union, that one has not penetrated the meaning of conjugal love. To give each other [95] a child is the married couple's sign that they really love each other, since they give each other mutually that which is able to fulfill their common life. The possibility — and the risk — that a child will be born from the sexual relation of the man and the woman should remind them that it is truly a human act, for which they assume the consequences in advance. We speak here of a risk because impregnation is not automatically tied, above all not in humanity, to sexual relations.

The deliberate and permanent desire to ward off the coming of children must be condemned as fundamentally selfish and sinful. But is the carnal union necessarily sinful when it is not accompanied in each case by the desire and the will to have children and if the man and wife, of common accord, agree about utilizing certain contraceptive methods to avoid the coming of children? The Roman

Catholic Church replies categorically yes and justifies its point of view by an affirmation that is quite well known. Pius XII expressed this viewpoint (following the traditional teaching, set forth notably by Pius XI in the encyclical *Casti connubii*, Dec. 31, 1930) in his address to the Congress of the Italian Association of Catholic Midwives: " The truth is that marriage, as a natural institution, is not ordered by the will of the Creator towards personal perfection of the husband and wife as its primary end, but to the procreation and education of a new life." [96] If this were the case, it would be necessary to reject all dissociation between the sexual life and procreation. But as we have already emphasized, marriage and the bond of sex find in mutual love their own proper meaning: the complete unity of the human couple is by itself in agreement with the merciful will of God. From the spiritual point of view there is no relationship of means to an end between the sexual relations of the spouses and procreation. The tie that relates them is more subtle: procreation is a blessing linked by a free divine decision to the formation of the couple.

There is nothing that is not legitimate in the desire of the couple, in a given case, to avoid the birth of a child and yet not to deny themselves to each other, so long as it is of common accord. In so doing, they bear witness that the act of bringing children into the world is a truly human act, intentional and carefully weighed.

Many reasons can lead the man and wife, in a given case, to avoid the birth of the child. Purely material conditions can legitimately intervene (e.g., insufficiency of resources, smallness of accommodations). Moreover, maternities that are too closely spaced can seriously impair the health of the mother, particularly her nervous system.

It even happens that the presence of children born previously can lead the parents to give up temporarily or permanently the idea of having more children, for the education of these first children would be compromised by more children. Can we say that in such a case the couple ought quite simply to abstain from sexual relations? This solution is frequently advanced as being ideal, but it is necessary to take into account human weakness, to consider that this voluntary abstention risks endangering the harmony of the couple, and indeed, inciting the husband to infidelity.

These arguments, which physicians, psychiatrists, and psychologists could support with numerous facts, are not without value. It is Christian not to presume too much of one's own strength, and it is certain that all individuals do not bear sexual continence with the same facility. But however valuable these arguments might be, they do not go to the very root of the problem: if it is true that the sexual embrace is a manifestation of true and total love, why should the reasonable decision to avoid the birth of other children or to delay the coming of a child be accompanied by a renunciation of this authentic manifestation of love? If one thinks so, is it not because one has implicitly already reduced the value of the sex act, because one has reduced it to a purely physiological function, and has dissociated it from the person by relating it solely to the species? Is it not because one considers the sex act as a sort of biological necessity, to which one must consent, but which is nonetheless a sign of our weakness and sin? Such reasoning would make it impossible to give a human meaning to the sexual life and to build an ethic of the sexual life.

The arguments raised by Roman Catholic theologians against birth control seem weak to us. They are encum-

bered by the initial mortgage of Roman Catholic thought,
that in the sex act the love of the married couple can be
only a " secondary " end.[97] Even more, the chain of reasoning is always based on arguments that are borrowed from
a philosophy of nature or a natural theology. It is thus that
Fr. Oraison writes: "An isolated sex act, willfully conceived as exclusively designed to manifest a mutual love,
and from which the fecundating power is deliberately
eliminated by a mechanical or chemical method, is properly speaking monstrous, i.e., it is foreign to the norm of
nature." [98]

Yet how can we discern a norm of nature? Are the
norms of nature as they appear in the economy of the Fall
intended by God? Can one not see in every sphere the indispensable evidence for counteracting the norms of nature, the dispensable justification for repairing the disorder
of nature, for limiting its violence? Has not man received
the vocation of gaining ascendancy over nature? [99]

We are not at all convinced when Fr. Oraison establishes a facile, but lame, comparison between a sex act
that avoids impregnation and a hypothetical act of eating,
viz., the act of chewing food while avoiding swallowing,
the act not having the purpose of nourishing the body.[100]
The two acts are not at all comparable because the act of
eating entails only a simple finality (it is necessary to eat
in order to live), while not only is the sex act a complex
in its finality but also it does not engage us alone: each
partner must have respect for the other, both in being con-
siderate of the other's pleasure and in taking into account
the consequences the other will bear. It is in this respect
that the "sacrificial" character of sexual love must be
manifested.

But another type of consideration seems to us to be

called for in the solution of this problem. It is a question of the person of the child. For the human being, there is no more contingent moment in his existence than birth. He is put into the world. He has not asked to live and to face a destiny that will perhaps be difficult or unhappy. Therefore we should do everything we can to see that the child is received in a favorable way. It is a duty of the social group to make provision for the accommodation and employment of children who are born, to prepare for them a social environment in which they will have a chance. But it is also and primarily the duty of the couple to receive the child in a good manner. The preparation of a layette and of a comfortable home is not all there is to it. The child must be well received morally, and for this he must be wanted. Experience proves that a child who has not been wanted, or whose arrival has even been feared, does not always find the welcome that is due him. This is true even when he lacks nothing materially, even when affection is not denied him. Quite often unknown to them, the parents can have an attitude toward the child that will make him, perhaps, a latecomer in an already numerous family, feel unwanted unless this feeling of not being wanted is transferred to an older child who is perhaps particularly difficult. Depth psychology has taught us that our conscious feelings do not make up the whole of our affectivity. The quality of the reception that we reserve for our children and the style of education that we give to them depend only partially on our will. A desired child has more chance of being happy than a child who has not been wanted. A child who does not feel fully welcome is in danger of having a difficult psychological evolution and finds himself exposed to more complexes than another. This is why it is so important that the process of impregnation be prepared by a free decision made in common by the parents to welcome the child, that the child be truly asked for in prayer. This is why it seems to us much better to speak of birth control rather than a limitation of births. This latter term has Malthusian overtones and can imply a real selfishness on the part of the parents, whereas birth control reminds us that bringing a child into the world is a voluntary act for humanity, an act of which we have weighed the responsibilities involved.

It is often in the most miserable and most degenerate social environments, among the least united couples, even in alcoholic environments, that the number of children is the largest and exceeds ordinary norms. What this means is that the parents are giving evidence of their incapacity to control births, that the act of procreation is for them tied to the sole fulfillment of a physical need, that sexual pleasure is sought in itself as a simple compensation for an existence burdened with many frustrations. The result is that unwanted children are brought into the world who are considered as an oppressive burden and who *are* an oppressive burden for a mother who bears alone the responsibility of raising them, and whose health is impaired by births that are too close together. To be sure, birth control is not a panacea. It does not make these homes happy. But at least it can make the life of the child less difficult, so that instruction on the methods of birth control, although forbidden by law in France, Italy, Spain, and Belgium, would be very advisable.[101] Such teaching is by no means inconsistent with the propaganda necessary for bringing about the real desire for the child.

There remains, obviously, the considerable problem of contraceptive methods, a problem that it would be wrong to consider as solely technical. The end does not justify the means. The Roman Catholic Church, always in the name of respect for the natural law, authorizes (outside of total chastity) only the use of the Ogino-Knaus law, which determines with some precision the periods of sterility of the woman (but these involve individual variables). More certain methods also exist for the determination of the periods of ovulation (the method of observing temperatures), but they presuppose minute details, leisure, and are scarcely useful except in well-to-do social circles. Methods that put the wife in physical or psychic danger must obviously be rejected (intrauterine impediments, vaginal injections, *coitus interruptus*). Methods must also be excluded that are not completely perfected scientifically and whose utilization could bring unforeseen consequences (contraceptive pills [102]). The only methods that can be recommended, outside of the observation of the Ogino-Knaus law, are those which are simple and safe (condom and pessary). It is difficult to see why these methods should be accused to being unnatural in an age where, in all spheres, technology has given us a legitimate hold over nature.

Only a physician can give sound advice concerning the use of these different methods.[103] What the moralist should say is that given the present state of our knowledge (and perhaps it will always be thus), the couple should always bear in mind the idea of the risk they must take, since no method is infallible. They should be reminded that even an unwanted child can be welcomed with gratefulness and that a believer is freed from all bondages, including those of the laws of depth psychology. This conclusion is not meant to destroy our preceding argument, but rather to remind us that although the married couple seek a sensible procreation, in order not to overestimate their strength, they never completely determine their future and that divine Providence can lead them in ways that they had not at all imagined.

It goes without saying that all recourse to abortion must be excluded from the perspective of birth control (except for absolutely compelling medical indications), for abortion, at whatever moment it is done, is an attack against the life of a created being. It is frightful to think that certain overpopulated countries, such as Japan, have been obliged not only to authorize abortion but to push it systematically.

To hinder the process of impregnation and to practice abortion are two radically different behaviors. Their very difference has led us to be very attentive to the singular gravity of an act — the sex act — that the majority of human beings perform completely without thought or self-control.

CHAPTER XII

Purity

BOTH FAMILY LIFE and the sexual life prompt a consideration of purity. This term is nearly always used in regard to the sexual life, which charges it with a quite negative sense that is regrettable.

First of all we will try to restore it to the fullness of its meaning. In the Biblical perspective purity is quite simply holiness, and this belongs only to God. Purity can come, then, only from God, for God gives that which he himself is. Purity is the very gift of God, which he gives us in his grace, in the revelation of his grace which is the Word. "You are already made clean by the word which I have spoken to you." (John 15:3.) For those who have received this Word, who have understood that it was addressed to them and that God was present for them in his Word, purity will consist in keeping themselves as the Word created them, pure and irreprehensible for the day of the Lord. In other words, it will consist in knowing that they are truly, through the promise given to them and in fact already, the temple of the Holy Spirit in their body and that all which they can do is to offer this body in living and holy sacrifice agreeable to God (Rom. 12:1).

Therefore, it is necessary to stop giving a negative sense to purity as something obtained by asceticism and essentially implying certain renunciations and prohibitions. In short, purity should not be considered as an endeavor to eliminate all Eros in ourselves and to await that ataraxy, that total absence of desire which Stoic as well as Epicurean wisdom (curiously coalesced against man) has presented to us as the supreme ideal.

For the Christian, Eros is tied to that vital breath we have been given, and holiness does not consist in the annihilation of this gift. This is why the Christian ethic turns its back on all systematic renunciation, unless it has a pedagogical significance (to teach us self-control) or unless it has as its object the good of the Christian. Any other renunciation would result in cultivating in us the desire of the flesh and its pride, in giving us the illusion of having accomplished a meritorious act: " Did you not die with Christ," writes Paul, " and pass beyond reach of the elemental spirits of the world? . . . Why let people dictate to you: ' Do not handle this, do not taste that, do not touch the other ' — all of them things that must perish as soon as they are used? That is to follow merely human injunctions and teaching. True, it has an air of wisdom, with its forced piety, its self-mortification, and its severity to the body; but it is of no use at all in combatting sensuality " (Col. 2:20-23, NEB).

At the same time that they reacted against these practices of mortification, the Reformers fought against monastic vows and especially against the monachal vow of chastity. Their reaction went well beyond the momentary significance that it had (the fight against certain abuses): it was a new notion of holiness and purity to which they wanted to give precedence. Indeed, it is not true that man is agreeable to God by voluntarily renouncing the gifts and the possibilities that God has offered to him and that testify to the inexhaustible generosity of the Creator. In particular, it is not true that the refusal of all sexual life is the equivalent of the purity that God requires of us. Although the temporal imminence of the Kingdom can, according to the apostle Paul, be reason not to found a household, it is nonetheless true that the man who marries, even in this hypothesis, does not commit a sin (I Cor. 7:28). It can seem wise not to marry only to the extent that this Kingdom appears to be quite near and because in this Kingdom one will no longer marry. But those who are already married should be quite certain that they are not required to renounce anything in their marriage and that they should continue to live as man and wife.

The solution to the problem of purity should not be sought on the side of abstention, but rather on the side of usage, of the liberty in the usage as Paul has defined it in I Cor. 7:29-31 and which he summarizes in this maxim: Let those who deal with the world be as though they had no dealings with it. This whole passage, to which we have already referred, can, moreover, be interpreted in the wrong way. In particular, if v. 29 (" Let those who have wives live as though they had none ") is detached from the whole, it can appear that this life is relegated to the ranks of inconsequential things, that the state of marriage must be lived as an adiaphoron, that while it is not necessary to break it off, neither is it necessary to take any account of it. This leads to the idea of an unconsummated marriage. Such is not the thought of the apostle, and the other examples prove it. For him it is a question of freeing us from the tyranny of the world, from Eros, from possession, from feelings, and from sexual desire. None of these things has absolute value. None of them can determine our existence. Our existence has found another center of gravity. It is completely consecrated to the hope of the Kingdom that comes. It is this hope that situates all other values in their proper place. It is not necessary to renounce but to utilize everything with this special liberty which the hope of the Kingdom confers. It is in this liberty that our purity will shine forth. It is our availability for the Kingdom that will determine our manner of using the creation and all its goods, including the spiritual riches that are offered to us.

Eros is not condemned; it is only illuminated by a new light, that of Agape which makes us see the other, the partner, as the person promised in the Kingdom of God. To the extent that *my* wife is no longer for me simply my wife but a fellow creature, an heir with me to the promise of the Kingdom, Eros can no longer be tyrannical, nor the sole source of inspiration for our attitudes.

We have said that there is purity when the Word is received by man. We can now add: there is purity when Agape is received into the bosom of Eros, when Eros, without ceasing to be what it is, accepts the finality of Agape. We have had to emphasize the complete essential heterogeneity of Eros and Agape, their radical difference not only in their manifestations but in their characteristic aims. But it would be wrong to infer from this difference that an encounter is impossible between them. The infinite qualitative difference that separates man from God does not prevent the encounter between God and man. And yet man does not cease to be man in this encounter. Because Eros is possessive, its own impulse is to transform other people into things. Impurity has its roots in this impulse. Sexual love knows the most conspicuous debasements, to be sure. But this is precisely because it is endowed with all the violence and all the seductions of

possession that have been created around it by a universe
shimmering with myths that mask the reality of the possessive impulse. The love that oppresses and the love that
prostitutes are two forms of the same debasement. Eros
should be stripped, not of its dynamism, but of its insidi-
ous will to capture. This will to capture results in debas-
ing, first of all, that which is the object of it, and in
turning, secondly, on the subject himself. This impulse
represents such a permanent danger that humanity has
never ceased, even in the midst of an aphrodisiac civilization, to develop the theme of love illusion, of love disen-
chantment, indeed, of impossible love. Sartre contends
that the very project of love is contradictory because it
wants to possess a person as such, i.e., with its liberty, and
that its aim is then that of an enslaved liberty.

The analysis on which this affirmation is based is assuredly correct, or rather, it would be correct if it were
truly impossible for Eros to be enlightened and transfig-
ured by Agape and if Agape were incapable of seizing the
dynamism of Eros in order to orient it toward generosity
and giving, i.e., toward purity. It goes without saying that
this victory of Agape is never established once and for all.
The conflict of Agape and Eros is never finished, and the
generosity of love always remains exposed to the suspicion
of inauthenticity. When love forgives, it can always be
wondered if this forgiveness is generosity or pride, as Gabriel Marcel has shown quite well in *The Man of God*.

Purity is never a state: it exists in man only as a goal.
But it is sufficient that this goal be present, that Agape
judge Eros, in order for us to be freed from the tyranny of
Eros. The experience of our failures in the search for a
pure love would be depressing if Agape were not an object
of hope for us, if we did not await the manifestation of

authentic man, i.e., if the hope of the Kingdom were not a conviction in us.

Only this hope can comfort us in the experience of our failures, in love's falling into the impurity of possession and the no less pernicious banality of habit. Only this hope can give to the encounter between man and woman a future beyond the satisfaction of the sexual act. The essential thing is not that purity experiences failure, but that there is a hope beyond the failure. Then the life in common, despite its difficulties and its crises, reassumes its character of joyous adventure.

This is to say that although the ethic of the sexual life can reject with impunity the counsels of wisdom, moderation, and self-control, it runs aground on the problem of purity. Only an eschatological hope that permits us to understand our failures, as well as our successes, as *signs*, as indications of expectation, can give a meaning to the search for purity. To be a person, to keep Eros from being an aberrant and depersonalized function, to love the other as a person, all this is possible only if we both know each other as joint heirs of the promise, only if we have both received the hope of the Kingdom, if we await the revelation of what we are. The common error of the church's preaching and teaching concerning love and marriage is that of making reference too exclusively to the Order of Creation, as if human events received nothing of their light from the future. Preaching on marriage should be eschatological, for otherwise it cannot speak of purity except as a virtue of renunciation and moderation, as the pale and somewhat melancholy virtue of a man who is settled, steady, and embourgeoised.

It is naïve to count on the institution of marriage alone in order to assure purity, as if the entrance into the state of matrimony had the power of purifying Eros. The Small Catechism of Luther, in its explanation of the Sixth Commandment,[104] is quite right in teaching that the problem of purity remains in its entirety after marriage. Indeed, purity appears in an even more difficult light; for marriage, because it creates a legitimate social order, can persuade us that it is enough for Eros to exert itself within legitimate limits, that Eros has as its object only one being and becomes at the same time pure.

Marriage in no way excludes sexual abusiveness. It circumscribes it within certain limits acceptable to society. In reality, marriage is often only a means of permitting Eros to give free rein to its possessive and tyrannical character until the day when it will deteriorate, by old age, into comfortable habit and when the man will be persuaded of his purity because he conscientiously fulfills what is called "one's conjugal duties." The sexual instinct that seeks only its own satiation is impure, even if it does not imperil the well-ordered society.

Even the mutual dedication of parents to their children does not purify their love. On the contrary, it can lead to the temptation for the man to consider his wife no longer as anything except the mother of his children. The departure of the children is a dreaded trial for many parents. It is no doubt a trial, but if it takes excessive proportions, is it not because the parents have ended up living only for their children? Is it not because they are in dread of finding themselves face to face with each other at a time when Eros has lost its vigor and has been transformed only by its growing old instead of by the Agape that would permit them to live in a personal communion? Between them Eros has become an annoyance: in its appeasement it remained impure. Although it is absolutely normal for the violence and jealousy of Eros to diminish, it is abnormal when there does not appear between the married partners a tenderness that makes love seem actually stronger than death, as the author of The Song of Solomon says (ch. 8:6). This passage makes a truly enigmatic statement. We know quite well that death puts an end to love, that death is what love dreads. This is true if love has not received the promise of a future, if love has been only sensual pleasure, if love has not created a bond of mutual belonging, if love has not built a new person.

Conjugal and family existence is a gamble. Marriage is an institution and family is a society subjected to rules that a more comprehensive society imposes on it. The purpose of these rules is to subordinate the married couple to the order of the more comprehensive society and to protect the social body against the impossibility and the violence of Eros. It is not certain that Eros will let itself be thus checked and that it will recognize in the limits imposed on it an opportunity and a chance to be fulfilled. The legislator cannot guarantee this. The happiness of Eros has its source only with Agape. This encounter is always an event, and an unfinished event. But when this event happens, the partners recognize within the institution a meaning that the legislator has not given to it and that is no longer compulsion but the freedom to give oneself in generosity, one to the other. Thus it is the exemplary likeness of the communion in the Kingdom. If Scripture accords to marriage, among all other human institutions, an exclusive privilege, if it compares the love of a man for his wife to the love of Christ for his church, it is because it well perceives that mysterious bond between conjugal union and the Kingdom, that prefiguration of reconciliation and of the final recapitulation, in this very humble, very banal, and very impure encounter of a man and a woman.

Notes

1. In the weekly *L'Express* of December 19, 1957.
2. The French example is particularly instructive. The Family Code elaborated in 1936 aimed at the protection and emancipation of the members of the family, and especially of the children, more than it concerned the family per se. The reactionary policy of Pétain, on the contrary, was pro-family from the start. The difficulties that governmental ministers and agencies have with regard to the family bear witness, even to-day, to the unsettled state of family policy.
3. TRANSLATOR'S NOTE. Mulhouse, in Upper Rhine, was long the center of the French textile industry. The owners of the factories pioneered in social reforms, notably the construction of workers' cities with low-cost housing and measures for accident prevention in the factories. Yet they maintained, in general, a patronizing attitude toward their workers. "This beneficent activity of the Protestant employers was not without a spirit of superiority and social segregation" (Emile Léonard, *Le Protestant français* [Paris: Presses Universitaires de France, 1953], p. 110. Cf. also P. Pflimlin and René Uhrich, *L'Alsace, destin et volonté* [Paris: Calman-Lévy, 1963], pp. 82–105).
4. Jean Lacroix, *Force et faiblesse de la Famille* (Paris: Editions du Seuil, 1949).
5. Martin Luther, *Le Grand Catéchisme* (Paris: Je Sers), p. 108.

6. As is known, the criminal code, which makes it obligatory to denounce a criminal to the law, excepts from this obligation anyone who is a close relation of the criminal. On the other hand, the Hitler regime organized the denunciation of parents by their children.

7. Charlotte von Kirschbaum, *Découverte de la Femme* (Geneva: Roulet, 1957), p. 31.

8. Cf. André Neher, " Le symbolisme conjugal: Expression de l'Historie dans l'Ancien Testament," *Revue d'Histoire et de Philosophie religieuses,* 34th year (1954), no. 1.

9. One will note, however, the singular evolution of family policy in the U.S.S.R. The Soviet state practiced a resolute policy of family dissolution from 1917 to 1926. From 1926 to 1936, its policy became one of neutrality regarding the family. Finally, since 1936 it has practiced a pro-family policy, characterized, on the juridical level, by the total suppression of divorce and by the repression of abortion (under pain of death). But this does not necessarily mean that it respects the family community per se.

10. Cf. J. J. von Allmen, *Pauline Teaching on Marriage* (London: The Faith Press, 1963), pp. 30–32.

11. The relative stability and imperviousness of the social classes has had, as a consequence, marriage within the social class. All other marriage was considered, and frequently still is, as a misalliance. Thus the family has been able, for a long time, to be considered as an essential guarantee of " the social order." But education and culture are beginning to cross over the bounds of the social classes. Young people of diverse social classes meet each other in school and university. From this comes the increase of marriages that no longer respect the law of social endogamy.

12. Naturally, in numerous individual cases the refusal of her femininity on woman's part comes from reasons of a psychological nature: unconscious resentment against brothers spoiled or adulated by their parents; complexes developed foolishly by parents who, wishing for a boy at any cost, cannot

console themselves with having a daughter and have treated her as the missing boy.

13. S. de Beauvoir, *The Second Sex* (London: Four Square, 1960).

14. André Schlemmer, *De l'Enfant à l'Homme* (Paris: Les Editions Ouvrières, 1958), pp. 118 ff.

15. Jean Cabries, in *Saint Jacob* (Paris: Plon, 1954), has admirably described the suffering and the moral impossibility of a bigamy taken seriously.

16. There is a profound truth in this affirmation of Geneviève Gennari: "The verity of a couple is that which outlives love " (*Journal d'une Bourgeoise* [Paris: Grasset, 1959], p. 53).

17. Let us refer here again to the fine book of Geneviève Gennari: *Journal d'une Bourgeoise*. If the marriage of the heroine was a disappointment, it is because, inflamed by the social questions, obsessed by a very realistic vision of the emerging nations and of the population explosion, she had wanted to militate for a political cause and found in her husband only supercilious and amused skepticism.

18. Let us remember that the child has made his entrance into literature, the reflection of the collective conscience, only with Romanticism.

19. Cf. Albert Sauvy, *La Montée des Jeunes* (Paris: Calman-Lévy, 1958).

20. TRANSLATOR's NOTE. "I will not die completely" (Horace, *Odes* III. xxx. 6).

21. Léon Blum, *A l'Echelle humaine* (Paris: Gallimard, 1945), p. 12.

22. Cf. René Fau, *Les Groupes d'Enfants et d'Adolescents* (Paris: Presses Universitaires de France, 1952).

23. It is difficult to understand why the Roman Catholic clergy, for obviously political reasons, encourages with some success in certain Protestant countries (e.g., the Netherlands) an excessive birthrate that results in very large families.

24. A. Sauvy, "La domination et le nombre des hommes," in *Diogène*, 1957, no. 3.

25. R. Debré, "La 'Famille heureuse' ou l'optimum fami-lial," in *Population*, 5th year (1950), no. 4, pp. 619–624.

26. TRANSLATOR'S NOTE. In the United States the status of women in the church is somewhat different, with certain de-nominations admitting women to all levels of ecclesiastical functions, including the ordained ministry.

27. Cf. Edmond Jacob, *Theology of the Old Testament* (Harper & Brothers, 1958), pp. 172–173.

28. Karl Barth, *Kirchliche Dogmatik* III/2, pp. 344–350.

29. A. Bouillard, *Karl Barth*, Vol. II (Paris: Aubier, 1957), pp. 255–256.

30. Paul Schemp, "L'Homme et la femme d'après l'Ecriture Sainte," *Foi et Vie*, 46th year (1948), no. 3.

31. Jean Hering is perhaps wrong in translating *doxa* by "copy" (*The First Epistle of Saint Paul to the Corinthians*, 1962, *ad locum*), for the term "copy" has lost some of its pungency and indicates a slight debasement.

32. Alain, *Idées* (Introduction à la Philosophie) (Paris: Hartmann, 1939), p. 339.

33. *Ibid.*, p. 341.

34. *Ibid.*, p. 345.

35. *Ibid.*, p. 345.

36. *La Femme. Ses modes d'être, de paraître, d'exister* (French translation, Paris: Desclée de Brouwer, 1954).

37. *Op. cit.*, p. 12.

38. S. de Beauvoir, *op. cit.*

39. This is one of the reasons why we cannot follow the Ro-man Catholic Church when it affirms that marriage contracted before the civil authority has no conscientious value for Roman Catholics. Whether it knows it or not, the state participates in the conservation of the creation. It is, according to Reforma-tion doctrine, the minister of God in its order. A marriage con-tracted before the civil authority is a true marriage and the church must teach this to its members.

40. Cf. J. J. von Allmen, *Pauline Teaching on Marriage*, p. 46.

41. Cf. Ph. H. Menoud, " L'image chrétienne de la femme," *Verbum Caro* (1950), p. 167.

42. Emile Pin, *Pratique religieuse et Classes sociales* (Paris: Spes, 1956), p. 409.

43. F. Boulard, *Premiers itinéraires en Sociologie religieuse* (Paris: Editions Ouvrières. Economie et Humanisme, 1954), p. 97.

44. Cf. the book of James Burnham, *L'Ere des Organisateurs,* translated from the English (Paris: Calman-Lévy, 1947).

45. *Esprit,* 21st year, Oct.–Nov. 1953. Article by Yves Grecques.

46. Whereas a four-room apartment built around 1870 had an area of about 325 sq. ft., less expensive apartments have seen, in France, their sizes go progressively from around 270 sq. ft. in 1947 to 210 sq. ft. in 1954 and even later in urban housing projects to 190 sq. ft.

47. Cf. Andrée Vieille, " Relations parentales et relations de voisinage chez les ménages ouvriers de la Seine," *Cahiers internationaux de Sociologie,* Vol. 17 (1954) (New Series, 1st year).

48. According to Philippe Aries, who made a survey on family consciousness on the plan of living conditions and the arrangement of rooms, even on the invention of the doorbell, according to religious and secular iconography rather than on legal instrument, family consciousness in France is of fairly recent date. The family is concentrated as a social group assuming total responsibility for the children only in the fifteenth century, and only among the bourgeoisie of the cities. In the seventeenth century it is still conceived of as something of "public nature." Around it lived an entire village of servants, friends, and clients, companions in the greatest promiscuity in the midst of the family dwelling, whose rooms opened on each other and were not specialized for any particular function. The family became a private reality, concerned with intimacy, only in reducing its size (communication to the French Academy of Moral and Political Sciences of Feb. 27, 1956).

49. These figures are borrowed from A. Girard (work of the National Institute of Studies and Documents of France, published in *Documents-Actualités de la Documentation française*, 1957).

50. This event, with incalculable consequences, is not very old. The organization of secondary education for females goes back in France to Jules Ferry and the aligning of this education with the education of males dates from the years following the First World War.

51. Although, as André Dumas points out, certain women have known, in the course of history, a " preferential emancipation," professional work is alone capable of modifying "the collective destiny of the female sex" ("Simone de Beauvoir et la révolte de la Femme," in the review *Foi-Education*, 31st year, no. 56, July–August 1961).

52. "Famille, société industrielle et démocratie," *Esprit*, New Series, Nov., 1960, no. 11.

53. In his survey in *Le Monde* (April 4, 1953), P. Drouin reported the following remarks received from an elderly deputy mayor of a village in the west of France, who was surprised to see that husbands and wives spent their Sunday afternoons together: "In my day this was fine during the engagement period. But once married the man left for the card party at the cafe, and the wife devoted herself to chattering with the neighbors or with taking the baby for a walk." On the collaboration of men and women, which is the object of present research of a department of the World Council of Churches, see the work of H. J. Rinderknecht, *Partnerschaft von Mann und Frau* (Zurich and Stuttgart: Flamberg Verlag, 1959).

54. TRANSLATOR's NOTE. An industrial suburb of Paris.

55. Cf. the report of Pierre Drouin, " Pour le meilleur et pour le pire," *Le Monde*, April 2–5, 1953.

56. Cf. J. Daric, " L'activité professionnelle des femmes" (census of 1946), in the review *Avenirs*, March–April 1951.

57. Colette Hovasse, *Difficultés de vivre* (Toulouse: Privat, 1960), p. 28.

58. The plan of part-time work has nevertheless already been adopted in numerous countries. In the United States, part-time workers are very numerous and their work has a permanent nature. In Great Britain (1955), 13 percent of all female labor in retail commerce is part-time work, 16 percent in restaurants and hotels, 13 percent in laundries, 11 percent in the medical services, and 12 percent in education. And in the period during and after the war (1944–1954), English industry had received the addition of a thousand part-time workers. Public powers have largely encouraged this type of work. Sweden and Canada have followed this example. In France, the Rueff-Armand Report (1960) recommended the formula. An opinion poll of the National Institute of Economic Statistics and Studies revealed (1958) that the number of women who would like to work, if less difficult conditions prevailed, reached 660,000. Statistics show also that in the United States, part-time workers are, in general, attracted toward the tertiary sector of the economy, toward office work and retail trade. Social protection is not impossible for women who work part-time, and who have the tendency to be exploited by employers under the pretext that they have other financial resources available: the law of Feb. 11, 1950, made provision in France for collective bargaining contracts for part-time women workers.

59. On the problems of the woman at work, on the prejudices that she encounters, on the adjustment of work to maternal duties, and on the conception that the woman has of her work, we refer the reader to the special number of the review *Esprit* of May, 1961, and in particular to the articles of Ménie Grégoire.

60. The number of youth contained in the youth movements is often ridiculously low. In 1960, French Protestantism counted some 70,000 young people between 17 and 25 years of age. But out of this 70,000 young people, 7,000 to 10,000 were contained in the youth movements and parish groups (Report of P. Nardin to the Protestant Youth Council, Dec. 1, 1959).

61. On the necessity of the welcome of the child by society,

see A. Sauvy, *op. cit.*, pp. 102 ff.

62. André Marchal, " L'action sociale face à l'évolution des structures sociales," *Action sociale et Service social* (Paris, 1955), p. 72.

63. Pierre Laroque, " Service social et Action sociale," *ibid.*, p. 25.

64. It is astonishing that the encyclical *Mater et magistra* (1961) continues to hold up family management, modified, it is true, by a cooperative organization, as the ideal to which Christians should attach themselves.

65. Cf. Jean Stoetzel's essay in G. Friedmann, *Villes et Campagnes* (Paris: A. Colin, 1953), pp. 355–358.

66. In the collective work *Laïcité et Paix scolaire* (Paris: Berger-Levrault, 1957), p. 282.

67. On the importance and the role of family atmosphere, cf. Colette Hovasse, *op. cit.*, in particular, Ch. VIII.

68. " In suffering," writes Paul Ricoeur, in commenting on Gabriel Marcel, " I suffer the very adherence of my body to myself." *Gabriel Marcel et Karl Jaspers* (Paris: Editions du Temps Présent, 1947), p. 103.

69. *Journal de Métaphysique* (Paris: Gallimard, 1927), p. 241.

70. P. Ricoeur, *op. cit.*, p. 98.

71. J. J. Rousseau, *Discours sur l'inégalité*, I, 85.

72. Cf. the book of Henri Desroche, *Les Shakers américains* (Paris: Editions de Minuit, 1955).

73. " La Sexualité. La Merveille, l'errance, l'énigme," in the review *Esprit*, November, 1960, no. 11.

74. *Ibid.*

75. Daniel Lys, " Le plus beau Chant de la Création," in *Etudes théologiques et religieuses*, 1958, no. 4, pp. 114–116.

76. Th. Bovet, *Le Mariage, ce grand Mystère* (Neuchâtel: Delachaux et Niestlé), p. 65.

77. Otto Piper, *The Biblical View of Sex and Marriage* (Digswell Place: James Nisbet & Co., Ltd., 1960), p. 48. (This book is a complete revision of *The Christian Interpretation of*

Sex, published by James Nisbet & Co., Ltd., 1941.)

78. Paul Ricoeur, "La Sexualité. La Merveille, l'errance, l'énigme," *Esprit*, November, 1960, no. 11.

79. P. A. Lesort, *Le Fer rouge* (Paris: Ed. du Seuil, 1957), p. 56.

80. Cf. Henry Leenhardt, *Le Mariage chrétien* (Neuchâtel and Paris: Delachaux et Niestlé, 1946). We follow his analysis of the Roman Catholic conception. In a recent book, Ernst Kinder (*Die Ehe*, cf. in particular p. 29) shows, with much persistence, that although the New Testament does indeed establish a relationship between marriage and the order of grace, marriage does not appear in the New Testament as a means of grace. Quite to the contrary, marriage has need of the saving powers of grace. Marriage is not the means of appropriating grace and salvation. It is the object of it, or at least a privileged object.

81. Who is able to decide if the forgiveness, in such a case, is an authentic forgiveness? It might be simply a form of pride, humiliating to the other more than allowing the other access to joyous liberty. Cf. the play by Gabriel Marcel, *Un homme de Dieu* (Paris: La Table Ronde, 1950, 2d ed.).

82. Karl Barth, *op cit.*, III/2, pp. 339–341.

83. Th. Bovet, *op. cit.*, p. 130.

84. On this point, see Th. Bovet, *op. cit.*, pp. 103–104, who underlines the necessity of being conscious of that fact that an erotic current continues to exist in these friendships.

85. We think these remarks are perfectly applicable to the pastoral household, which too often suffers from a permanent invasion of members of the congregation and which, because of this, progressively loses the virtues that it should have.

86. It is a fact that widowers always marry wives a great deal younger than themselves, whereas during the time of their youth they wished to marry someone from their own generation.

87. Cf. Th. Bovet, *op. cit.*, p. 11.

88. *Petition*, XXXIII. Text quoted in Max Thurian, *Marriage*

and Celibacy (London: SCM Press, Ltd., 1959), pp. 53–54.

89. TRANSLATOR'S NOTE. The standard French Protestant translation of the Bible (Segond) follows a variant reading of the Greek text at this point. Cf. the marginal notes for the passage in *The New English Bible*, Library Edition.

90. M. Thurian, *op. cit.*, p. 114.

91. *Ibid.*, p. 50.

92. Karl Barth, *op. cit.*, III/4, pp. 156 ff.

93. TRANSLATOR'S NOTE. The French Protestant monastic community near Cluny of which Max Thurian is a member.

94. Marc Oraison, *L'Harmonie du Couple humain* (Paris: Les Editions Ouvrières, 1960), p. 60.

95. We readily use this unusual expression. The current expression is that the wife gives her husband a child. This adequately expresses masculine pride, since the man considers himself as the sole head of the lineage. In reality, the gift is mutual and it should be. The man and wife fulfill each other together in the person of the child.

96. TRANSLATOR'S NOTE. *Vegliare Con Sollecitudine*, published in *Acta Apostolicae Sedis*, Vol. xxxxiii, 1951, num. 17–18. Translation of Catholic Truth Society, London.

97. Cf. M. Oraison, *Vie chrétienne et Problèmes de la Sexualité* (Paris: Lethielleux, 1952), p. 204. This book, despite its quite traditional positions, was condemned by Rome and withdrawn from circulation.

98. *Ibid.*, p. 206.

99. See the arguments to the contrary developed by M. Oraison, *L'Harmonie du Couple humain*, p. 65.

100. The idea of natural law weighs very heavily upon all Roman Catholic thought in this area. "The purpose of nature expresses the will of the Creator," the Sovereign Pontiff declared in a letter addressed to the Social Week of Palermo, 1953. "The Church recognizes in these natural structures a value that transcends the power of human liberty and love." (Fr. S. de Lestapis, *Points de vue sur les Problèmes de Population* [Paris, 1950], p. 19.)

101. Concerning the happiness of the couple, let us mention, without attaching an absolute value to it, the famous survey made in Indianapolis on the relation between family happiness and a determined planning of births: 45.2 percent of households having always been able to avoid undesired births were found in the category "happy," whereas only 17 percent of the households that had had children without having wanted them were found in this category.

102. TRANSLATOR'S NOTE. For a recent evaluation of the safety and reliability of the various contraceptive methods, especially intrauterine impediments and contraceptive pills, cf. W. D. McElroy, "Birth Control," *The Johns Hopkins Magazine*, Vol. XIV, no. 7 (May, 1963), esp. pp. 37–38. Reprints available from the Legislative Reference Service of the United States Congress.

103. We refer to the book of Dr. H. Fabre, *La Maternité consciente* (Paris: Denoël, 1950).

104. TRANSLATOR'S NOTE. Seventh Commandment according to the Reformed tradition.